# Geometric Designs to Color

## volume 1

original designs by Brooke Snow

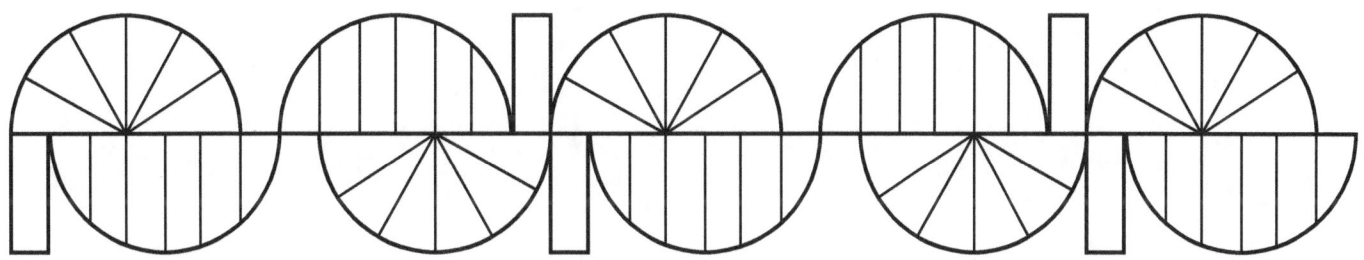

This coloring book will work with crayons, pens, colored pencils, markers, dried berries crushed into a fine powder and pressed into the pages with your finger, etc.
Etc.

Keep in mind though, that some media such as markers, may bleed through these pages.

To prevent this from messing up the page behind it and causing a fit of anger which completely ruins the whole **"relaxing effect" of coloring,**
use a blotting page or rip out the blank page at the end of this book and keep it under your artwork as you color.

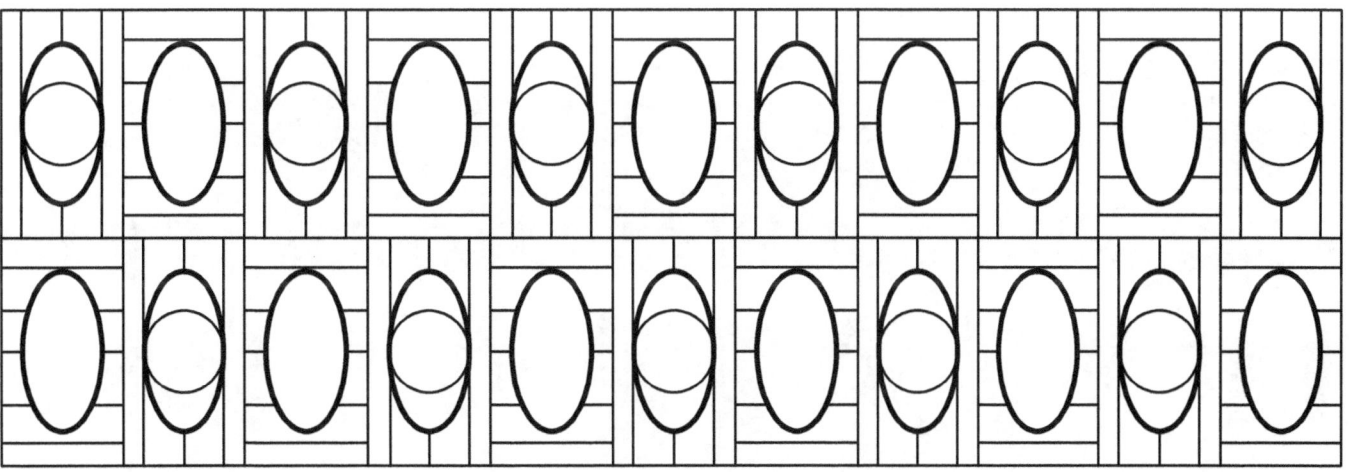

Colored a page you adore and want to share it with the world?

Use **#coloredunsurly** and your finished artwork may end up in the gallery!

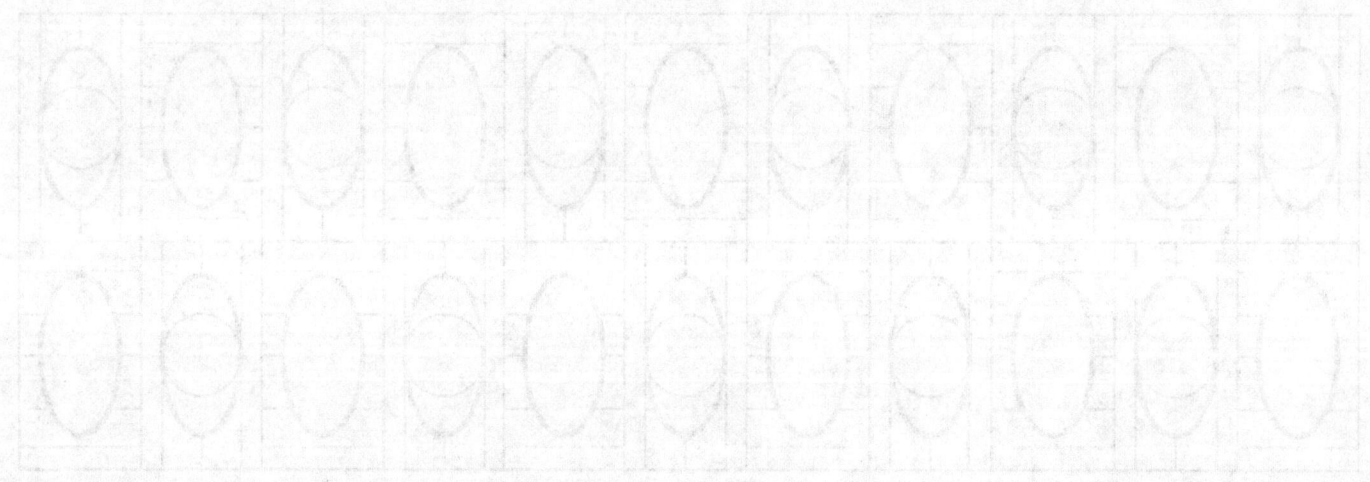

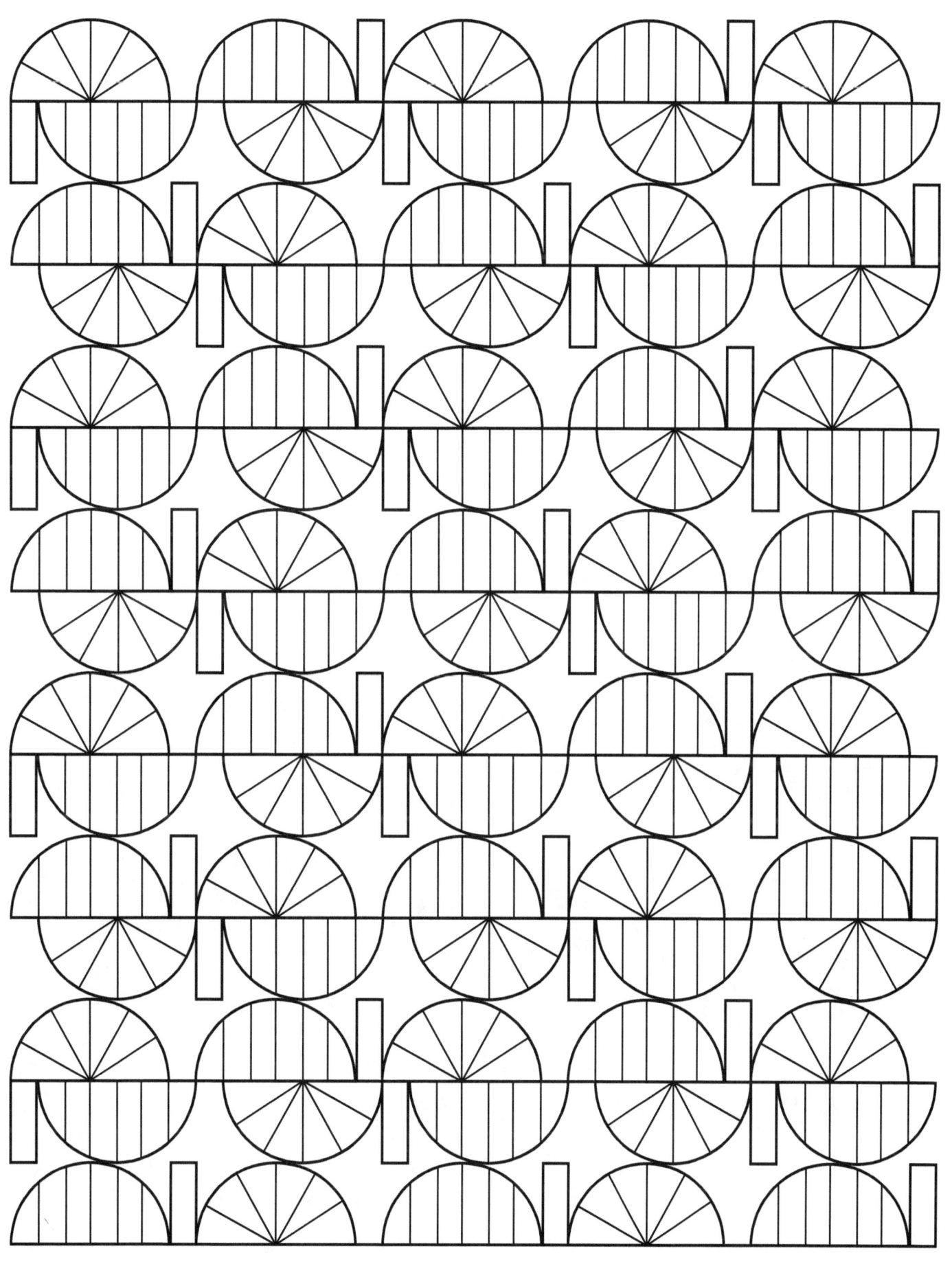

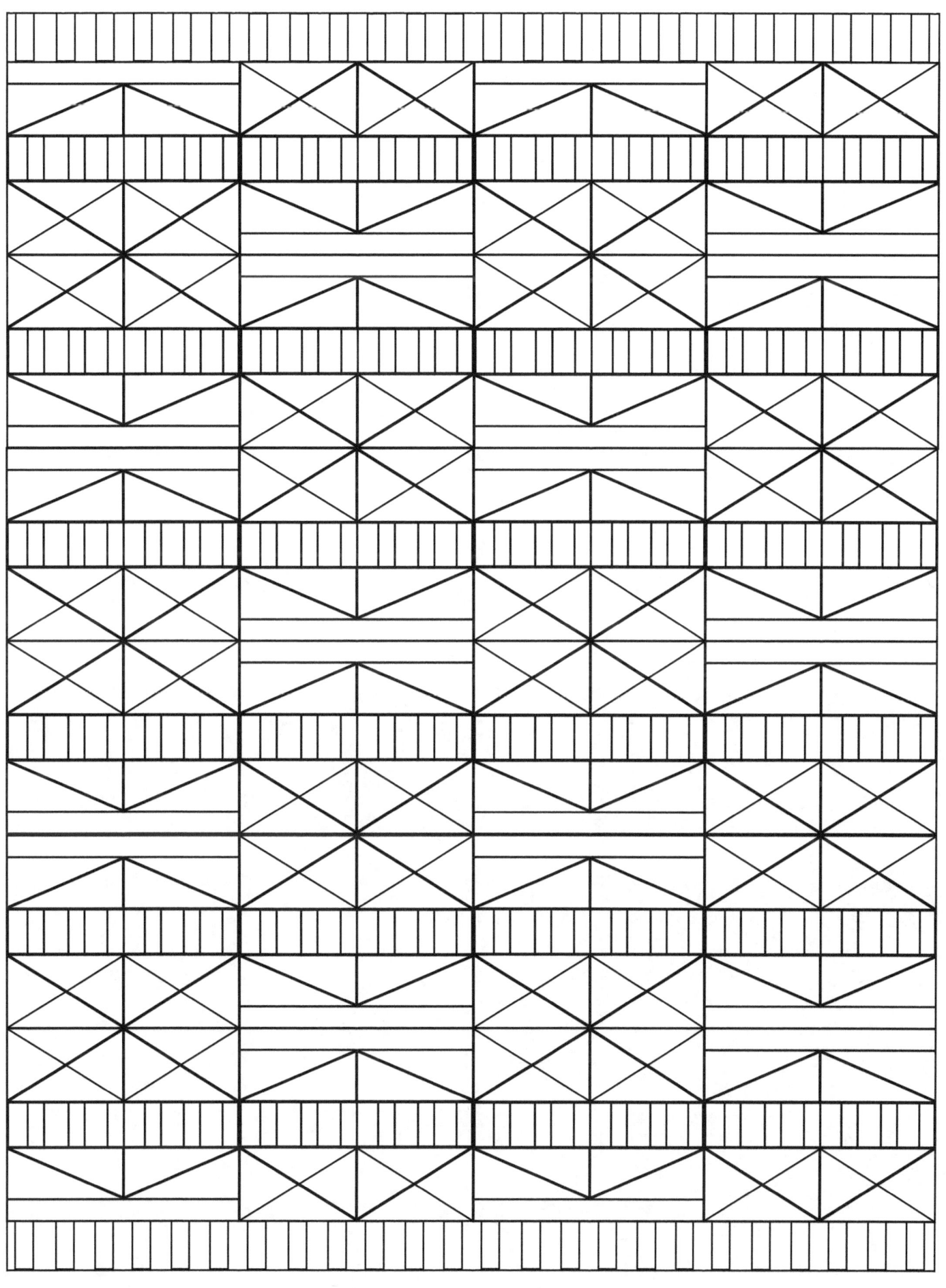

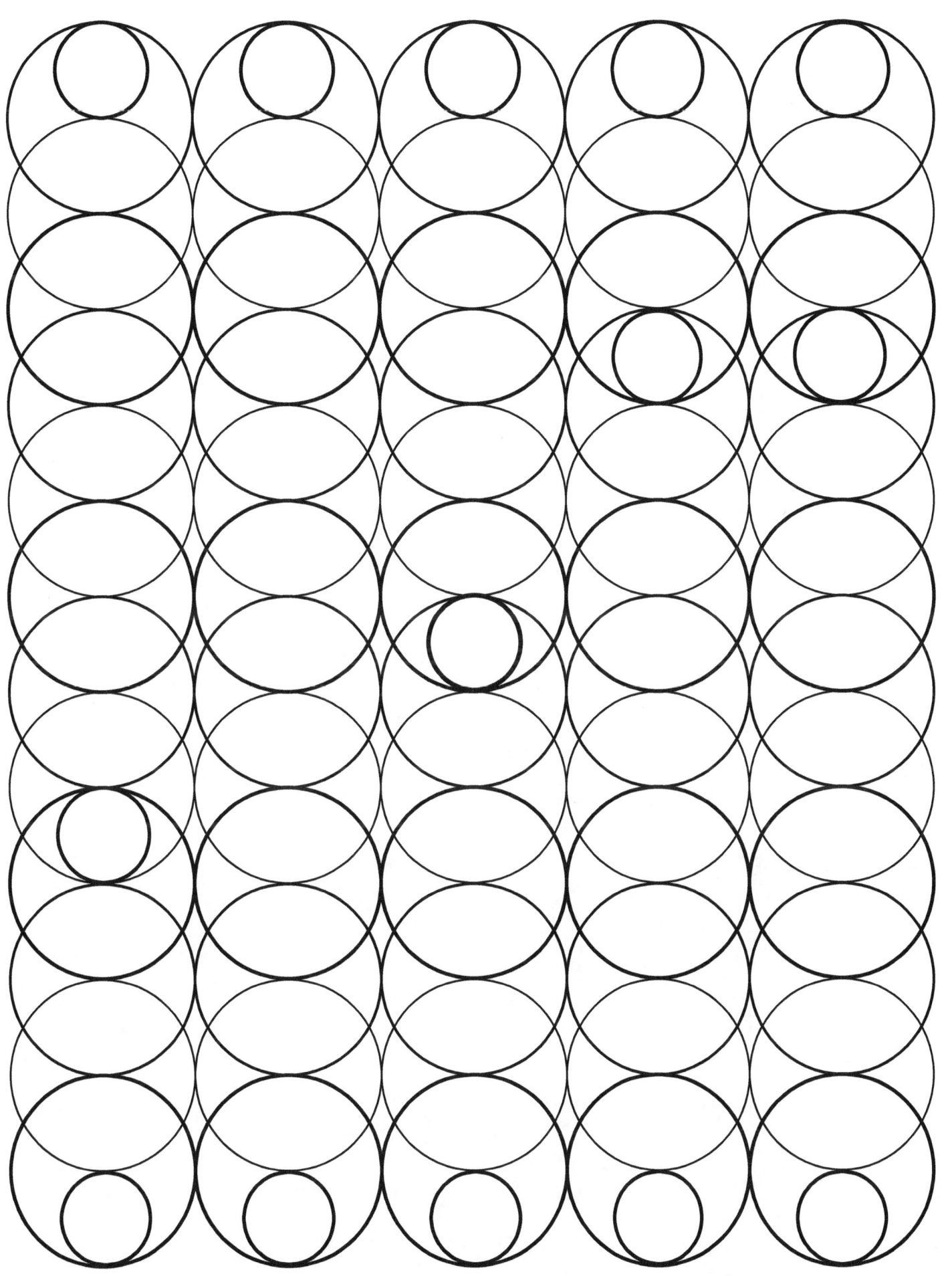

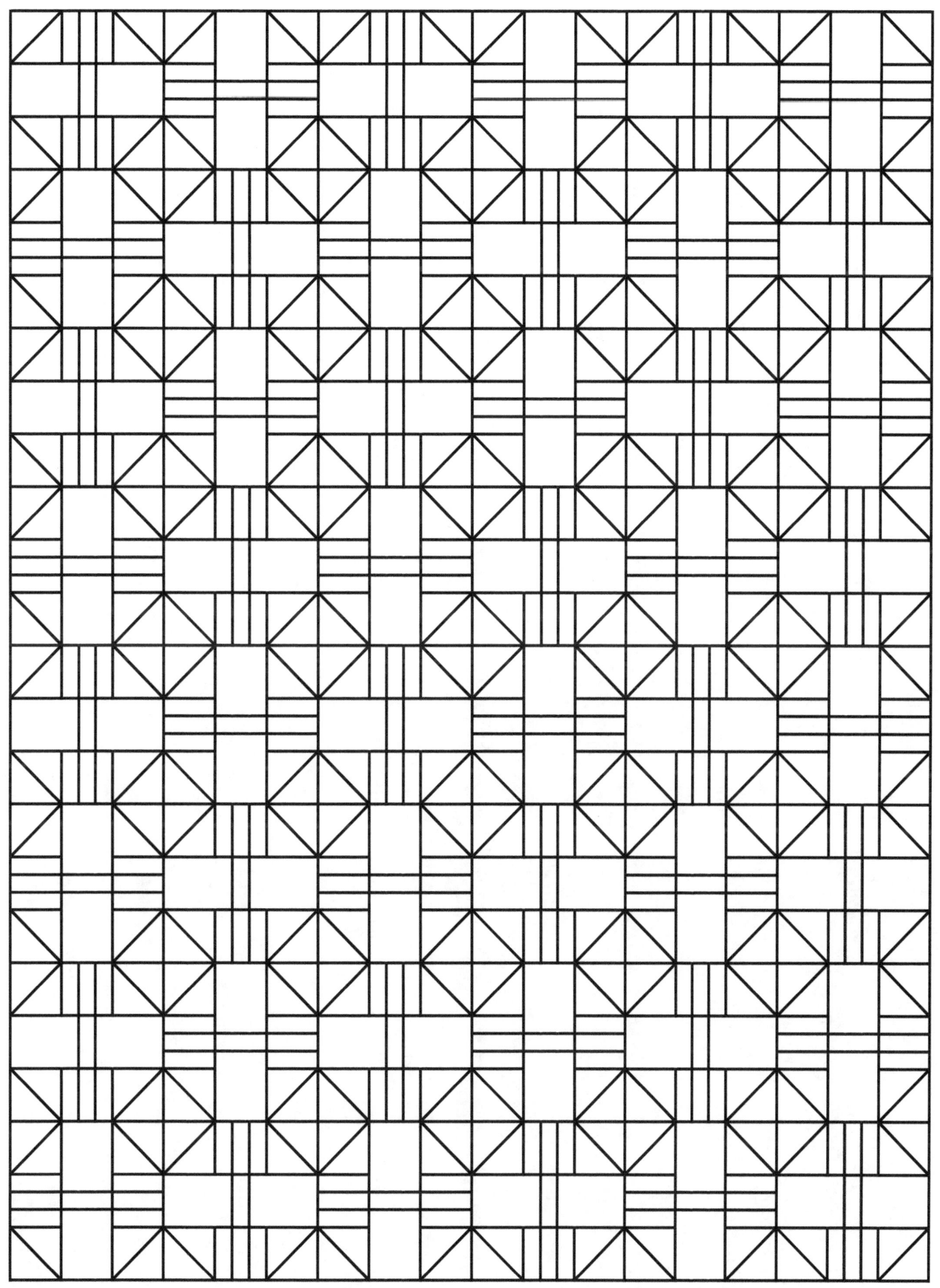

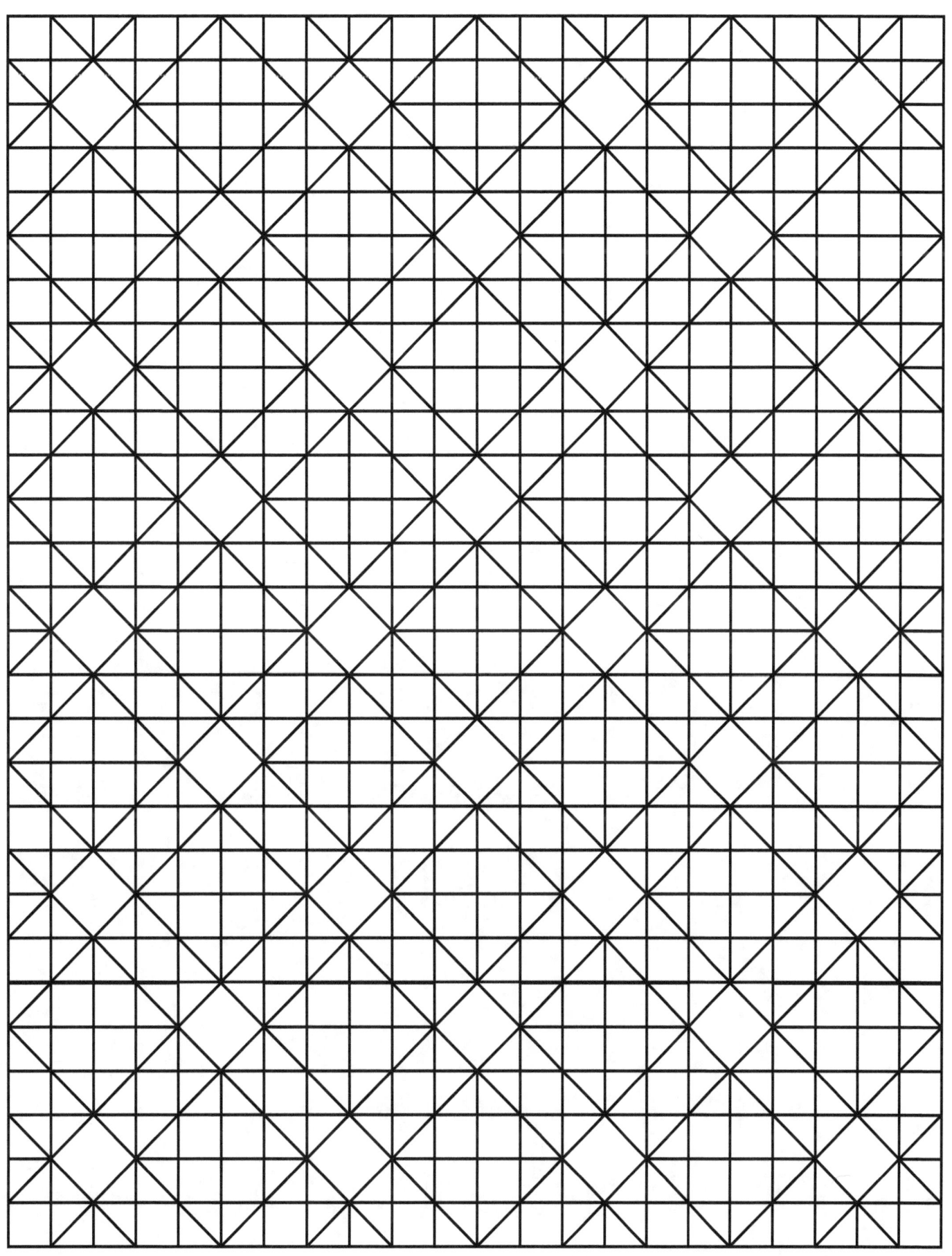

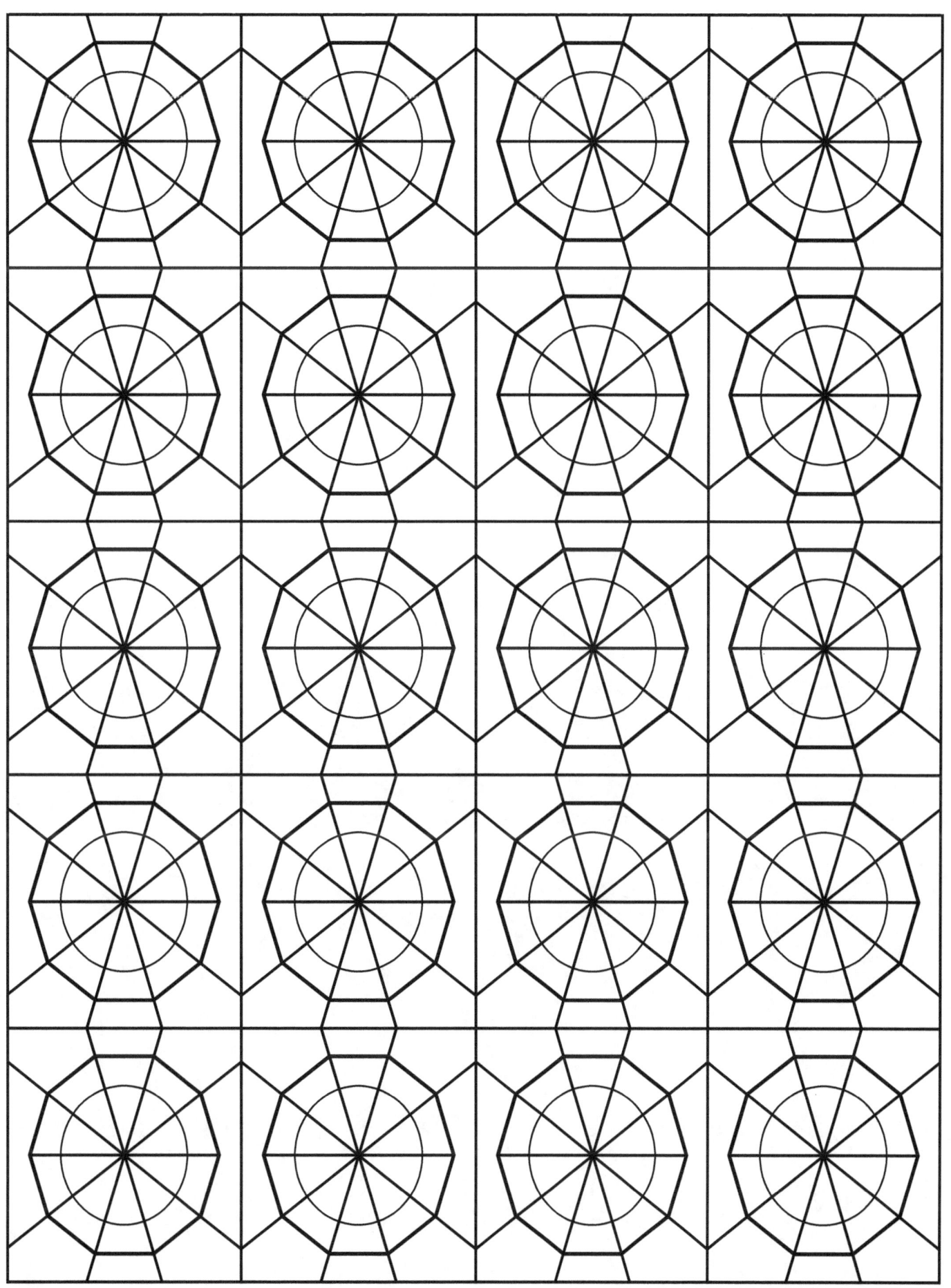

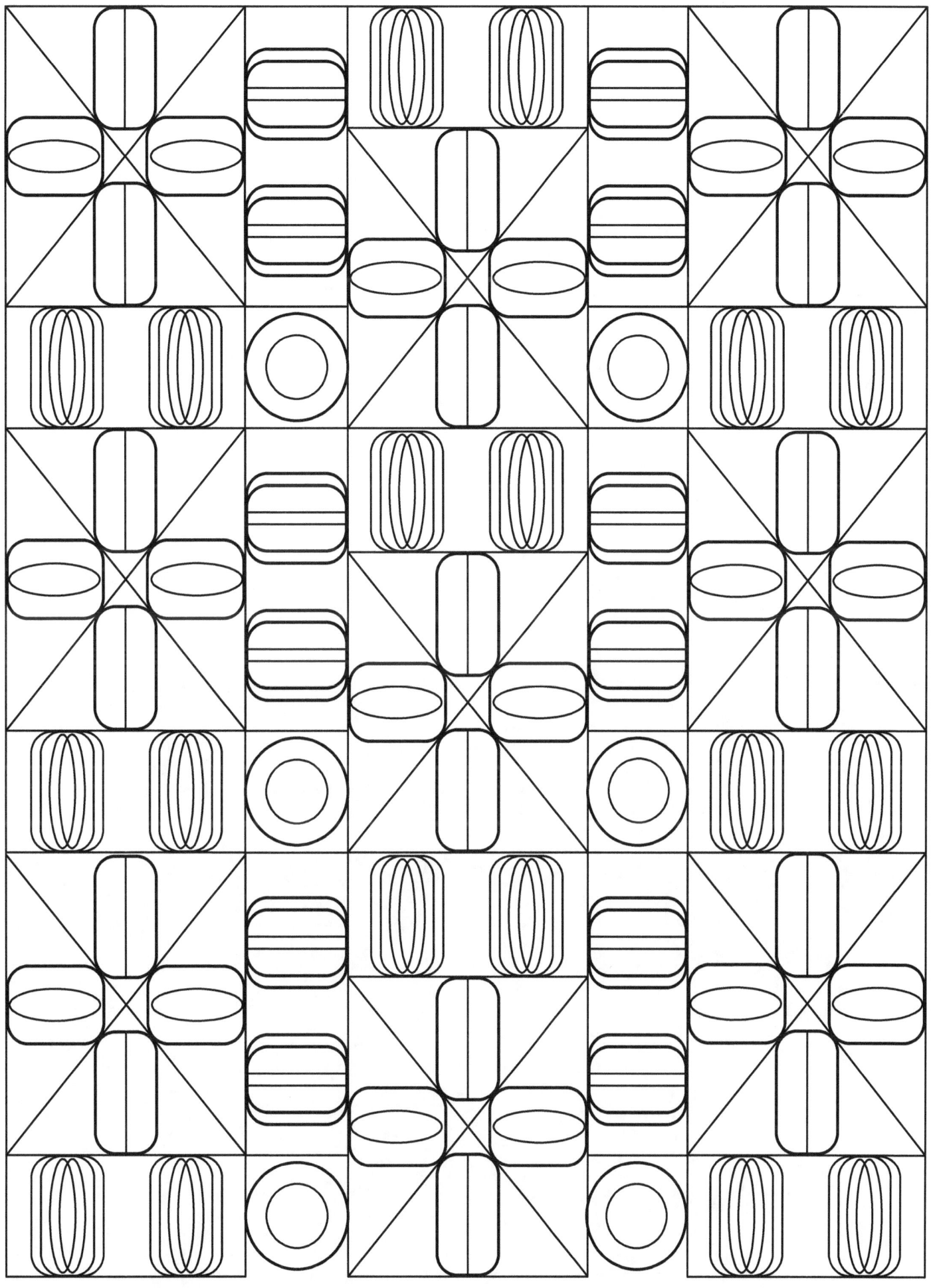

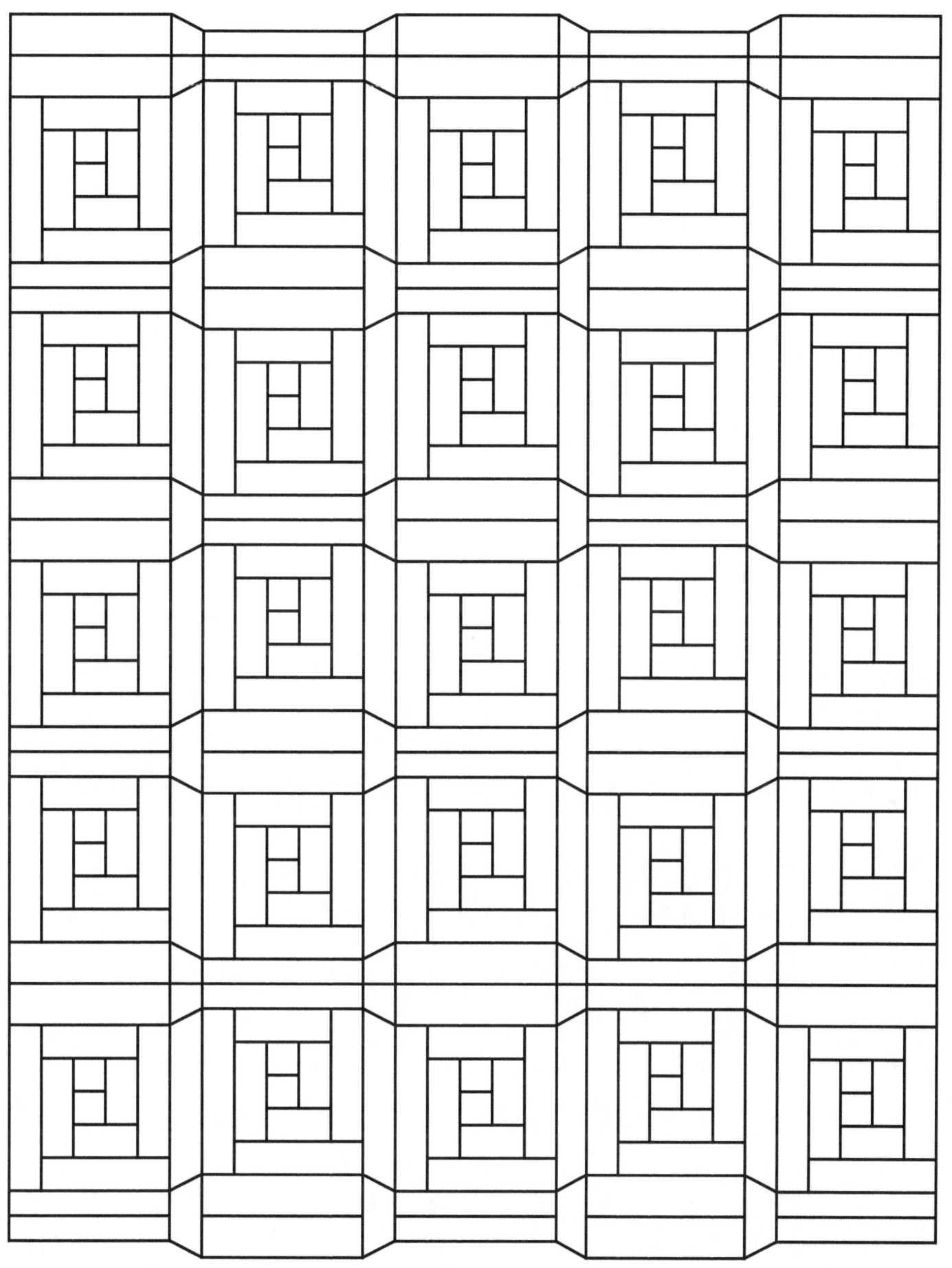

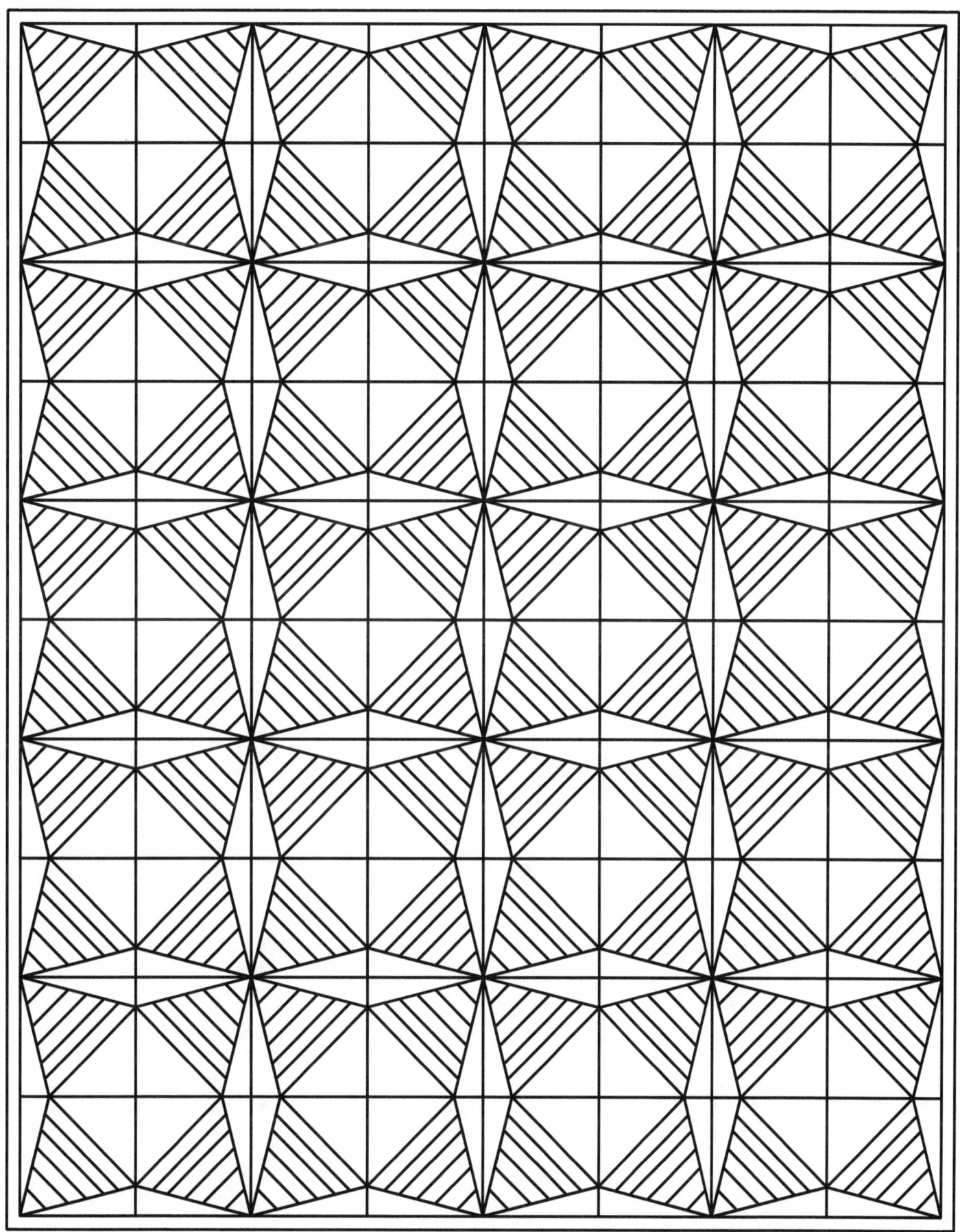

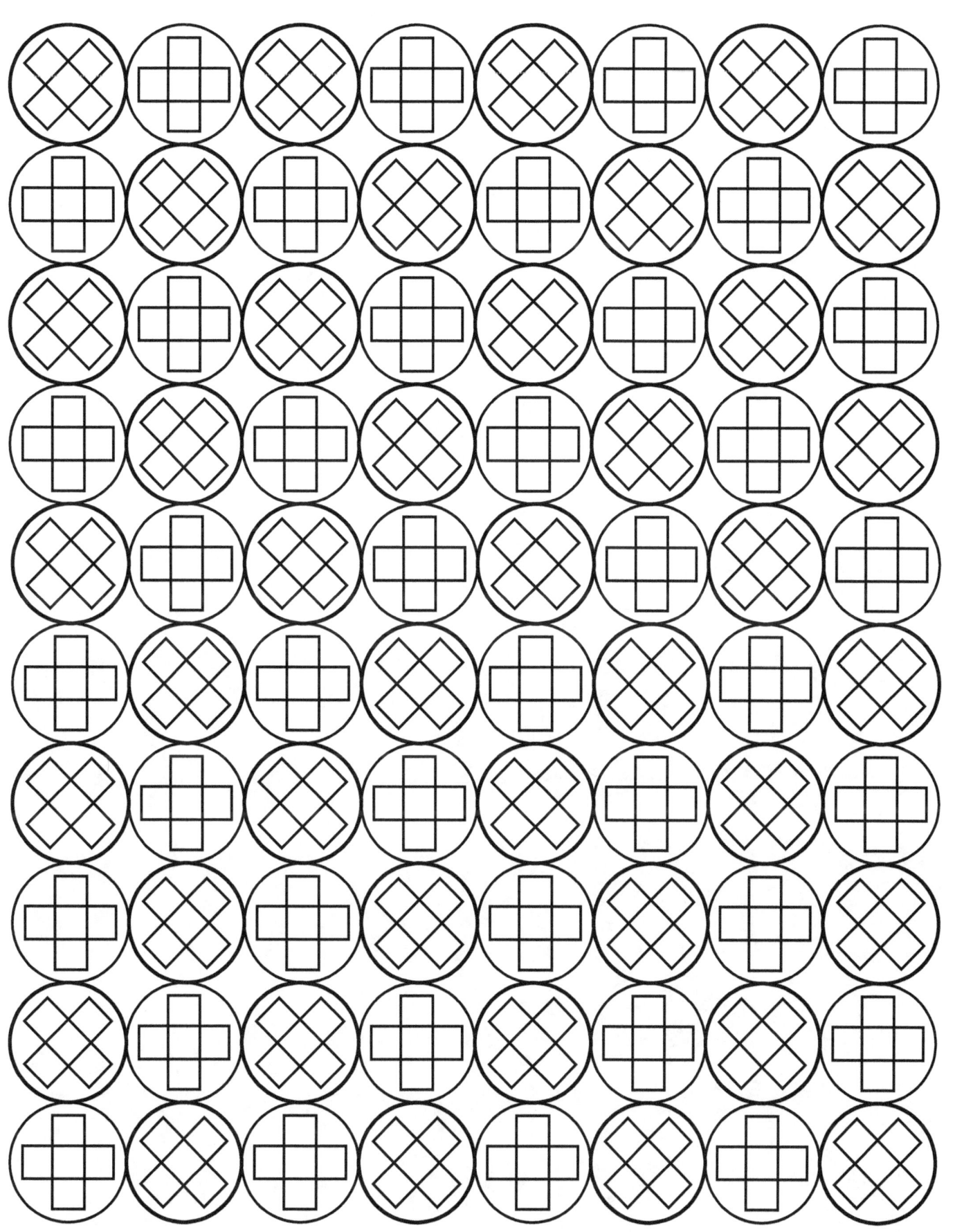

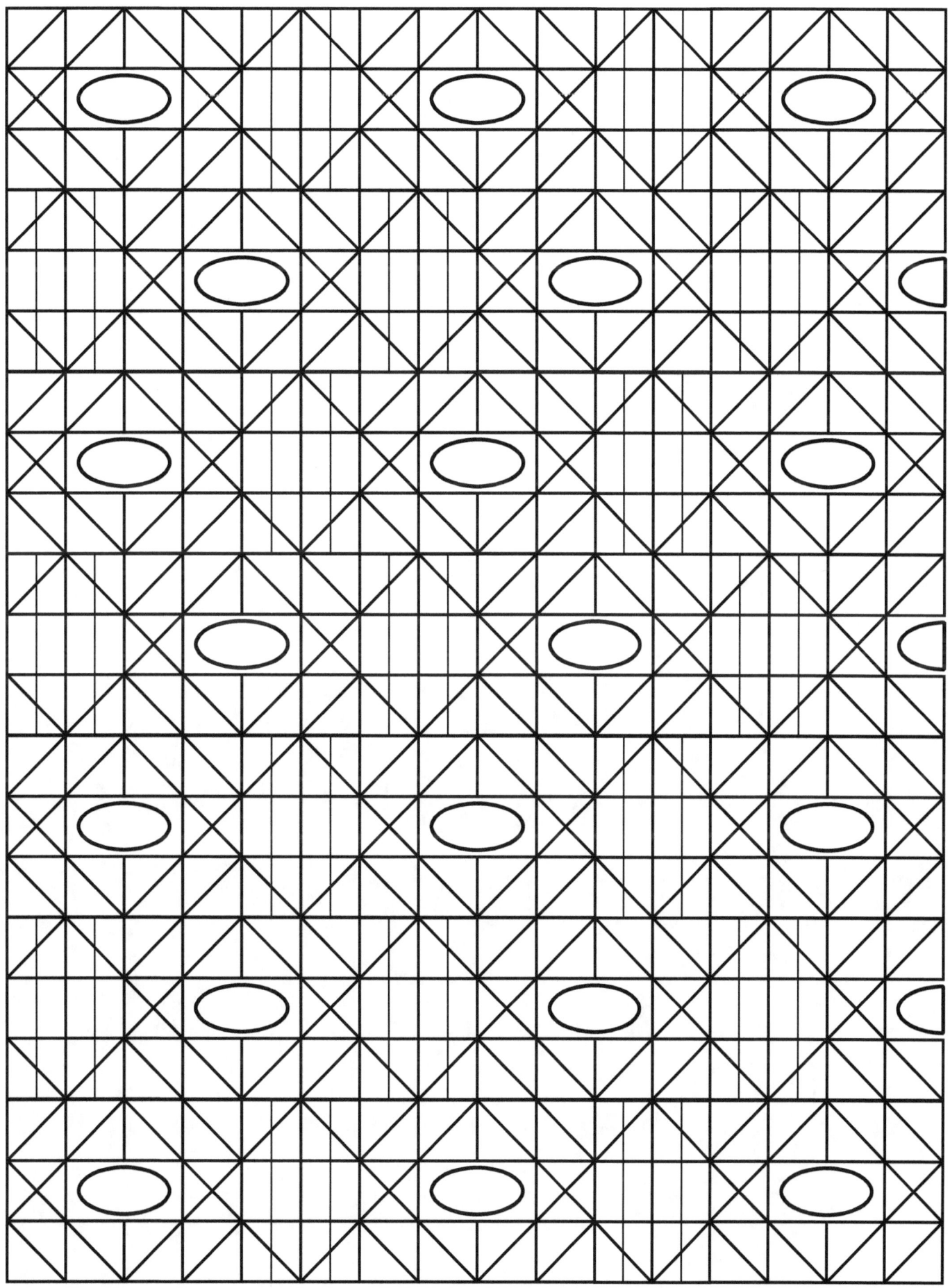

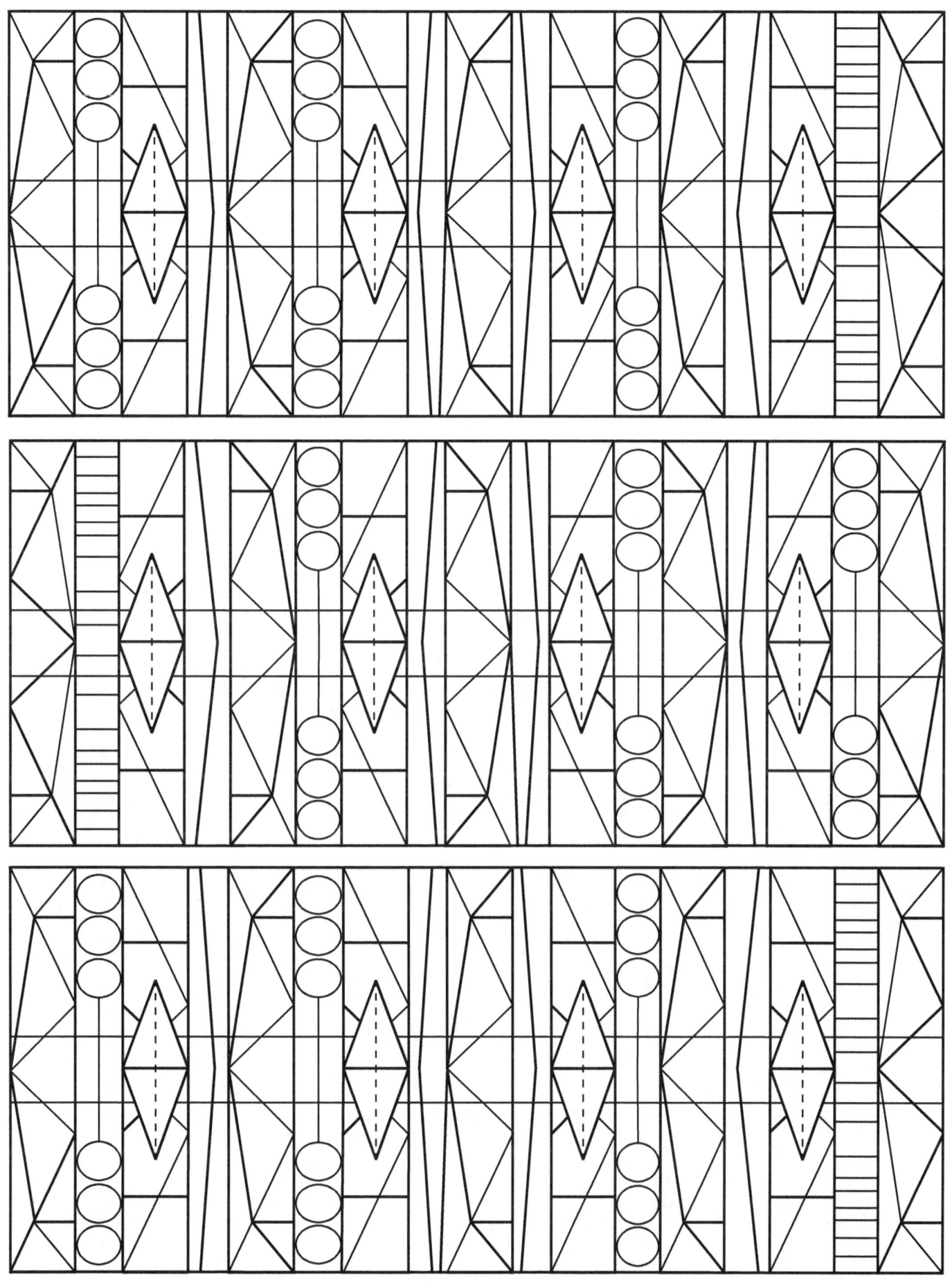

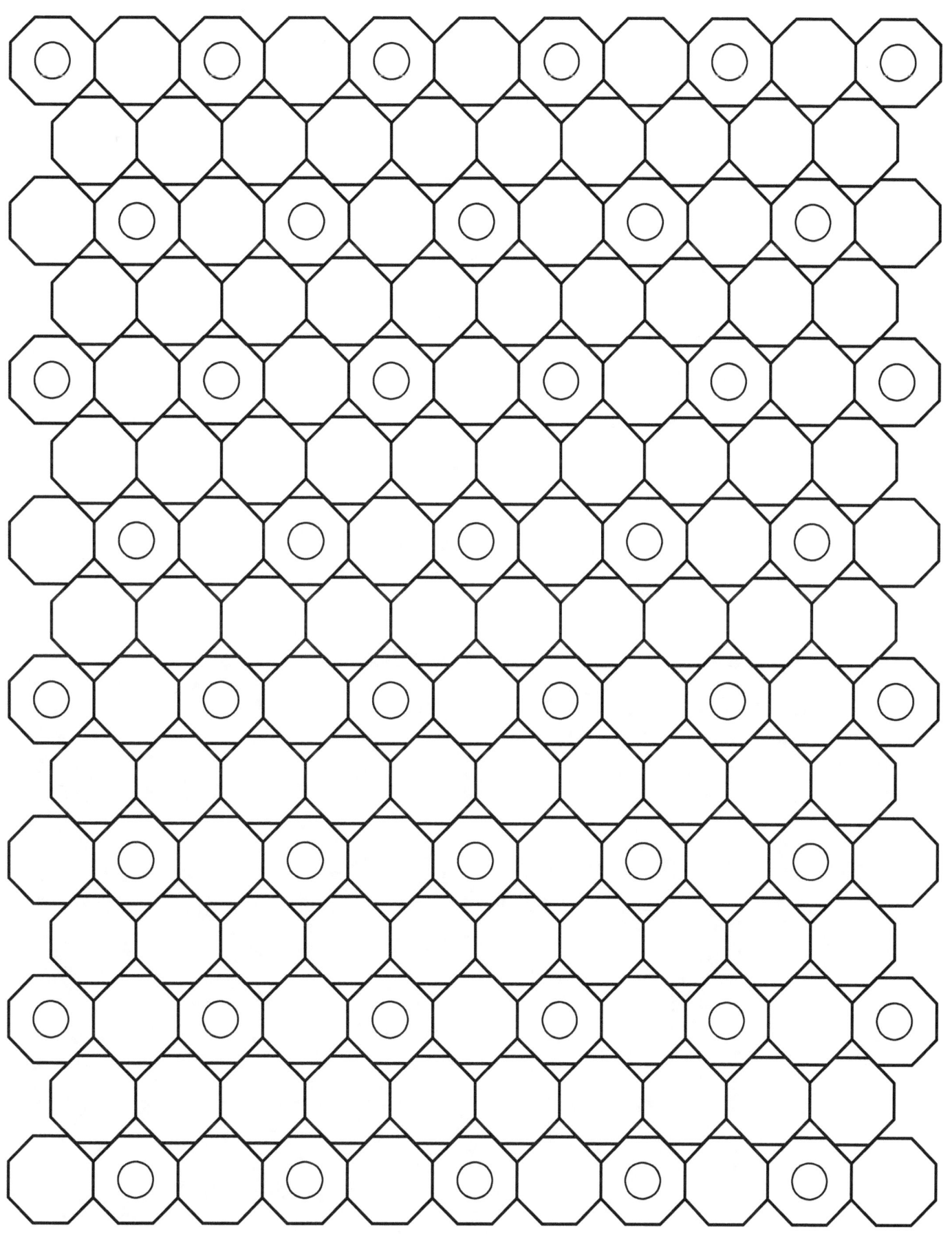

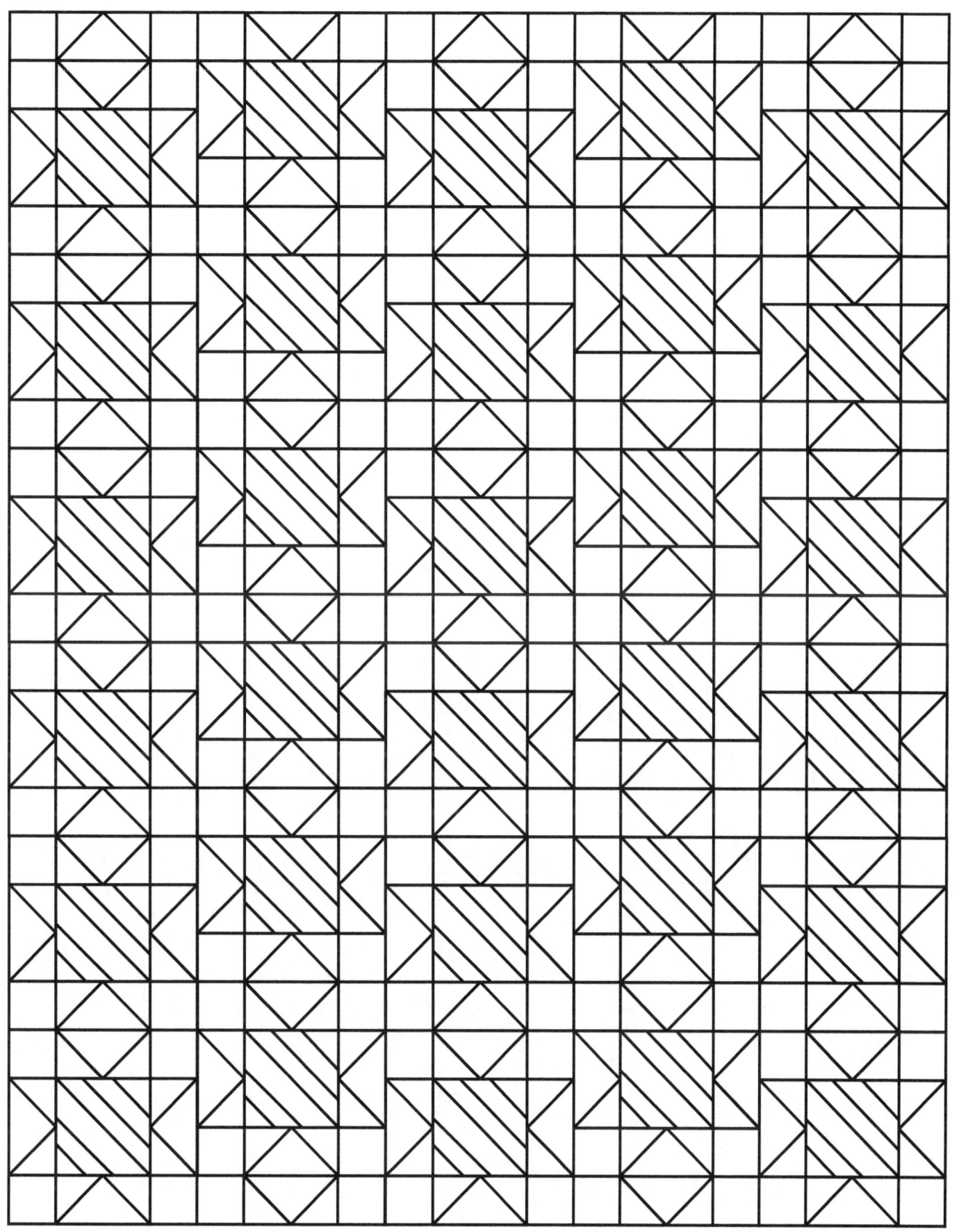

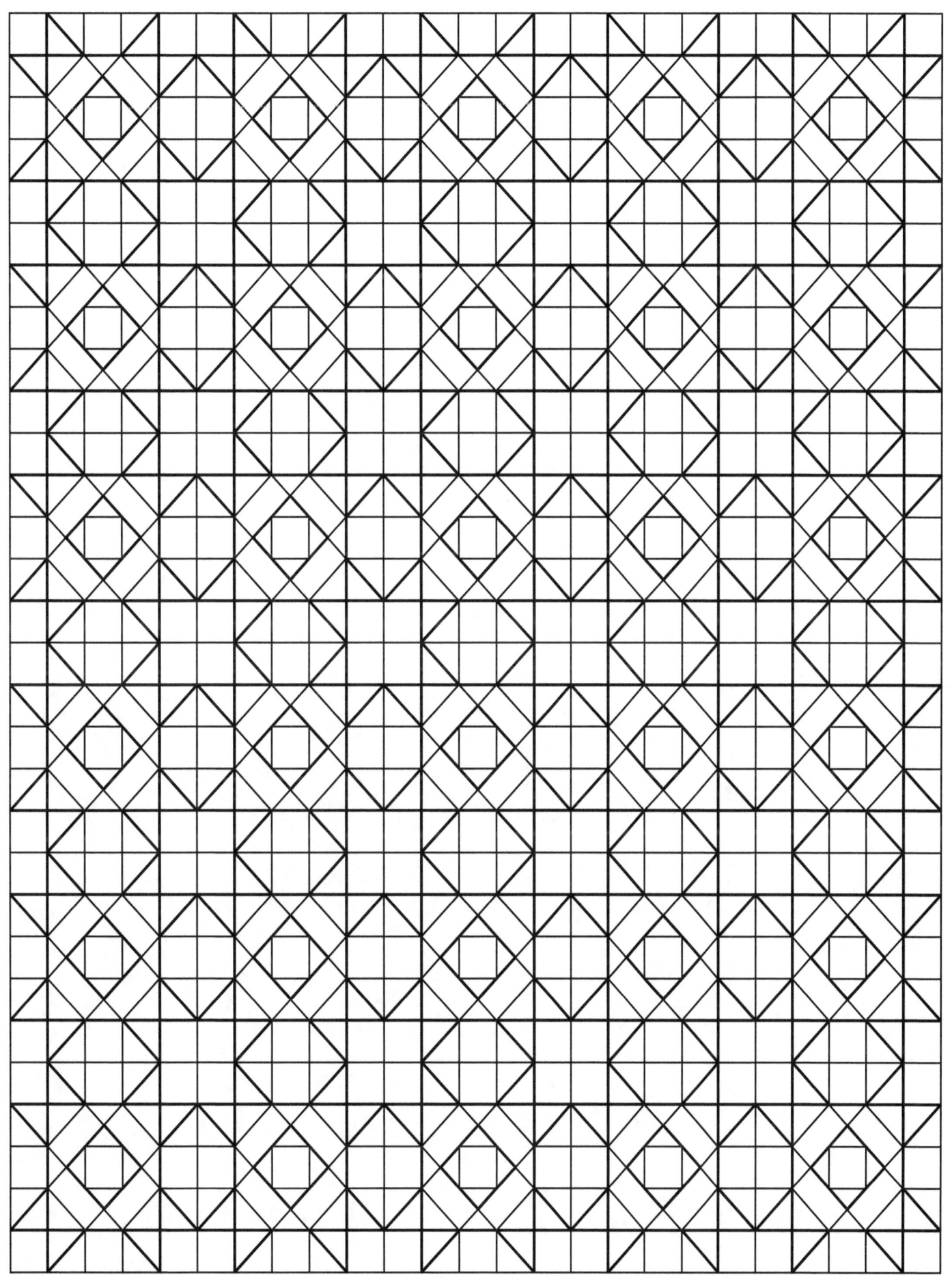

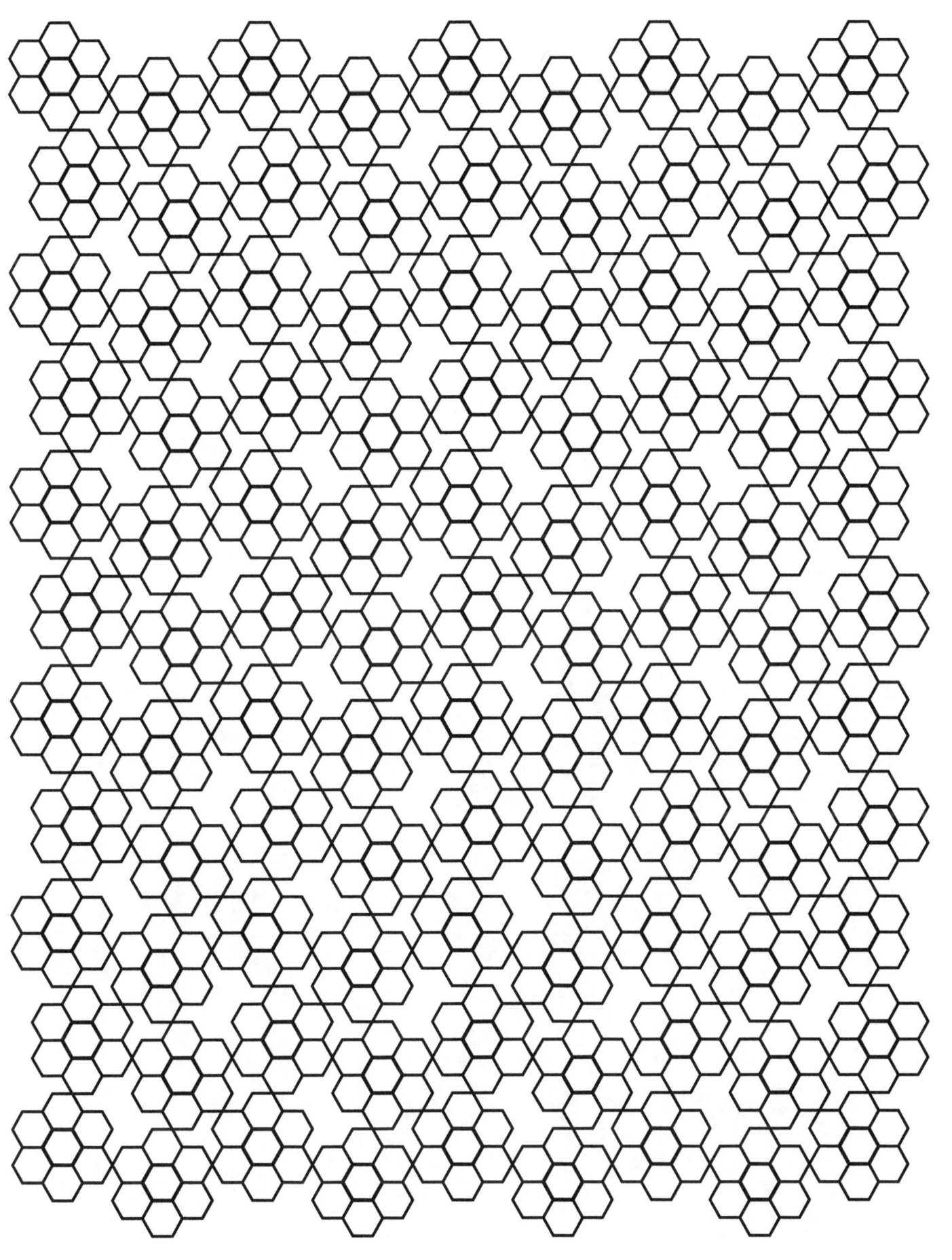

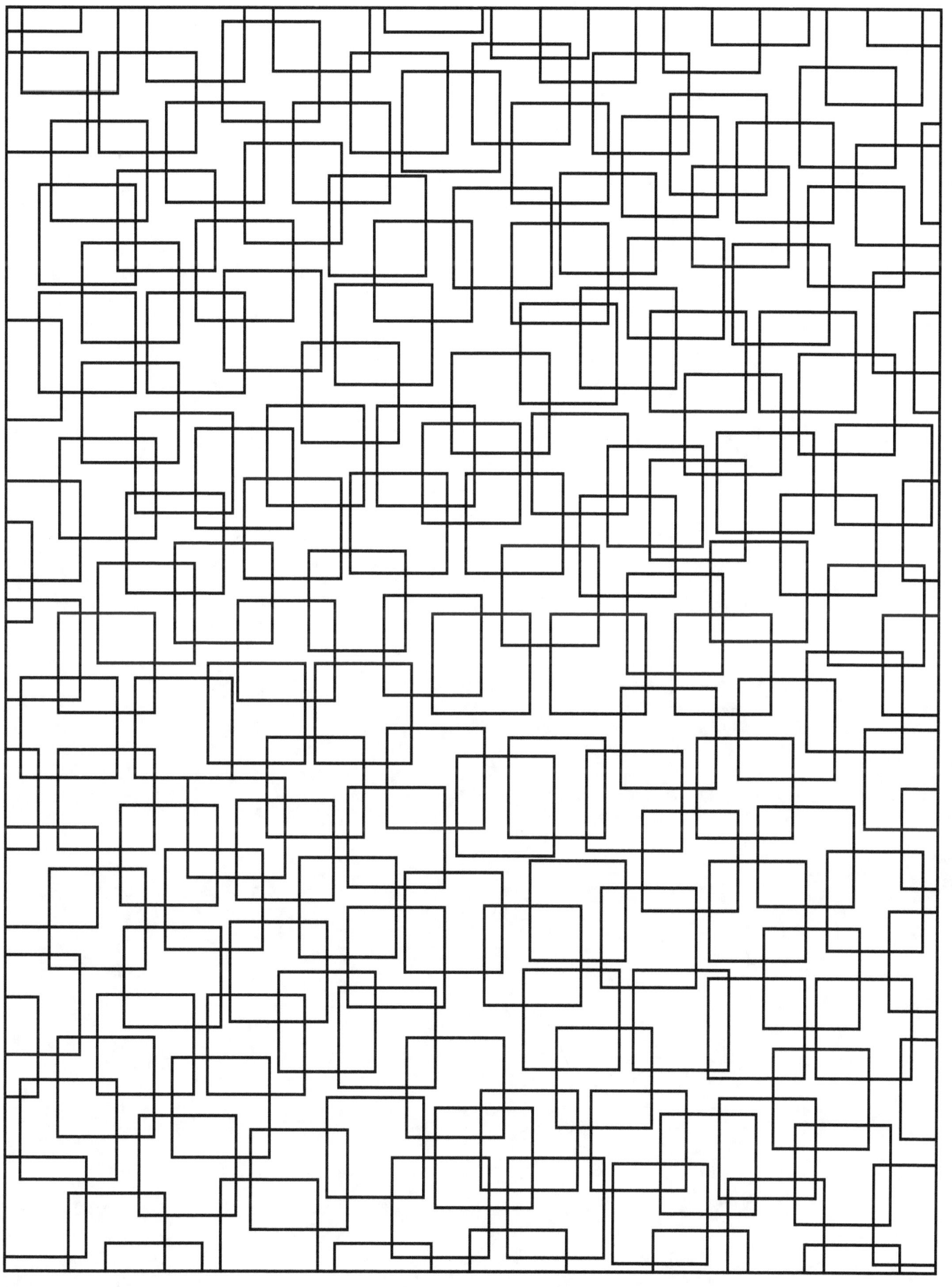

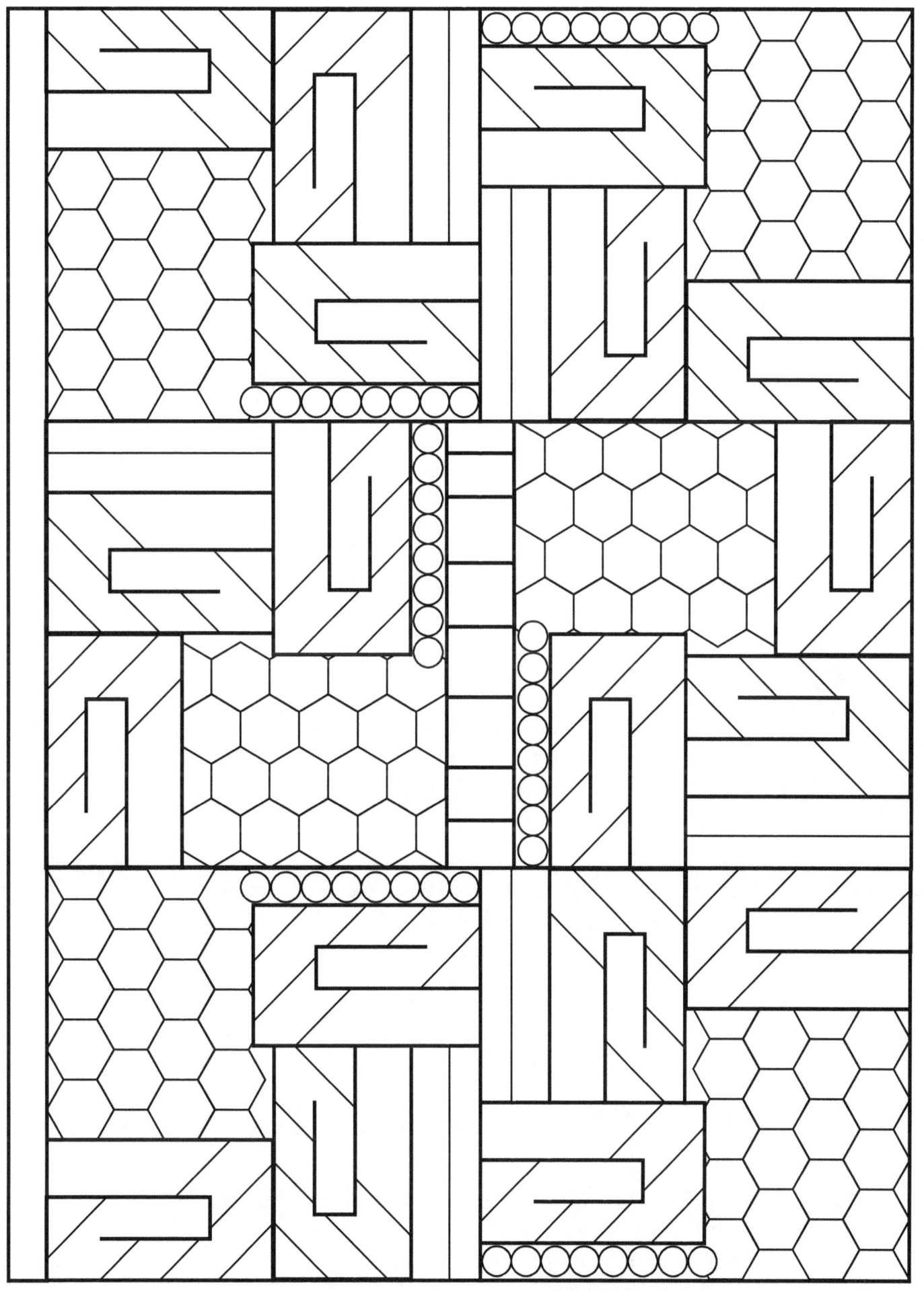

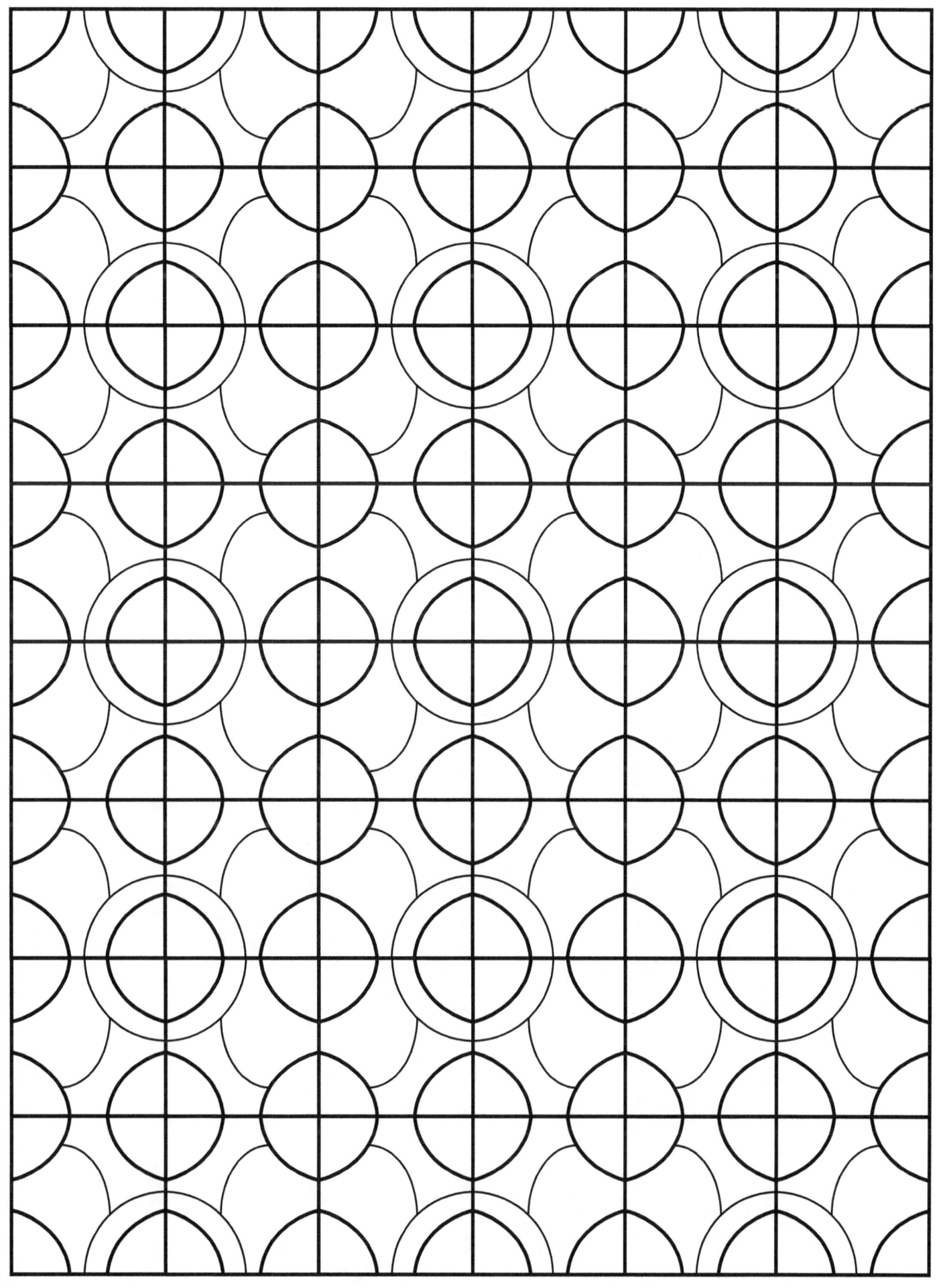

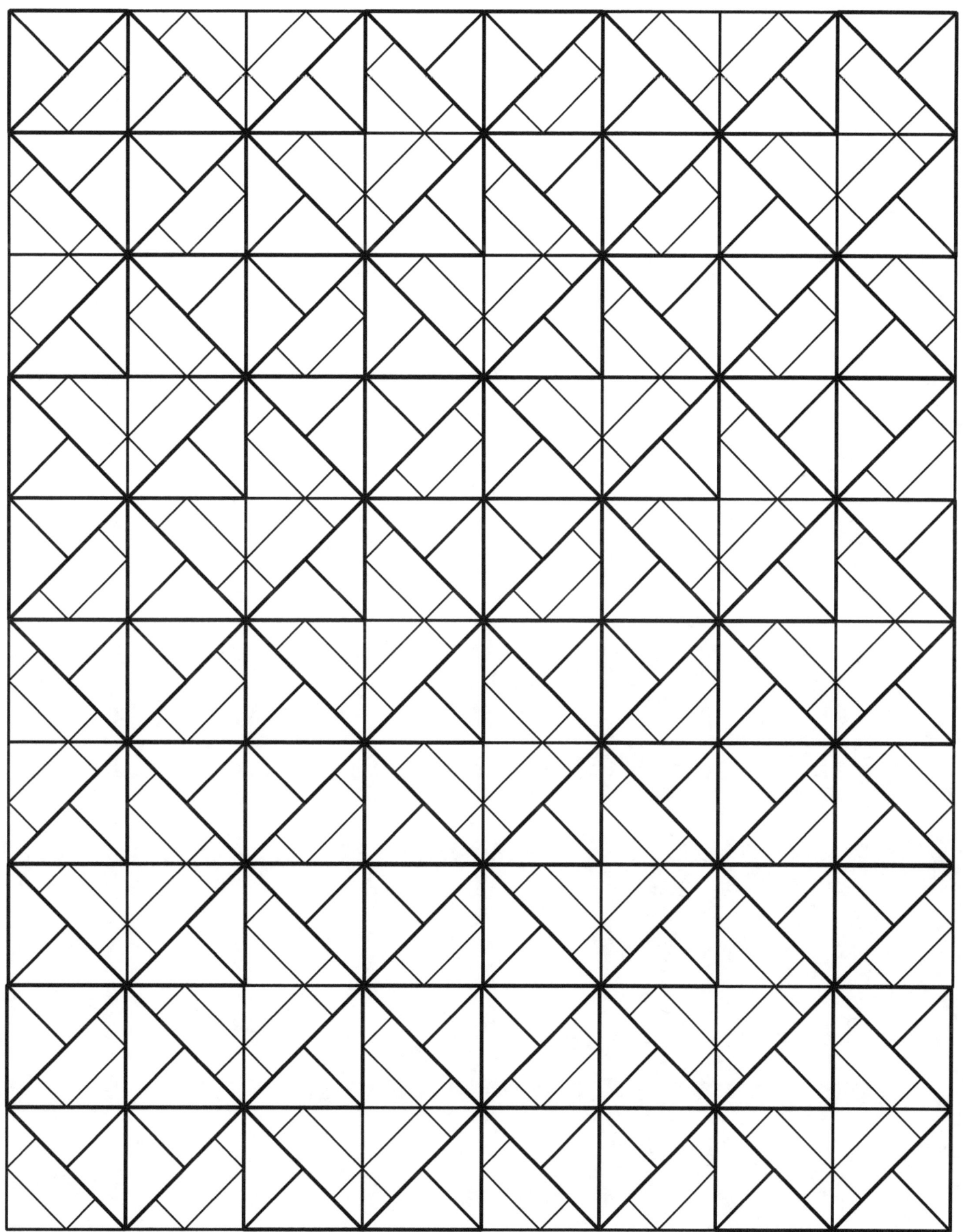

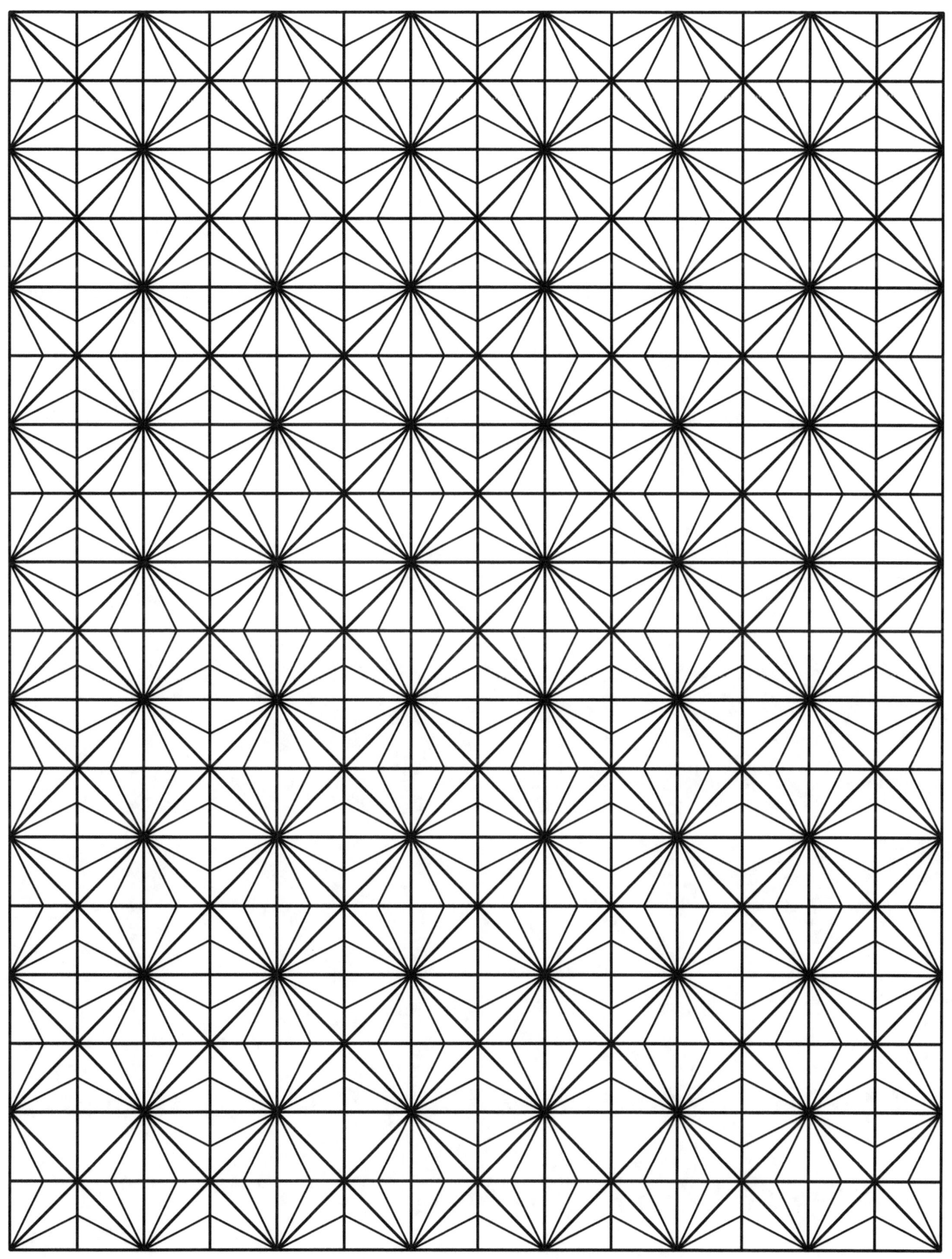

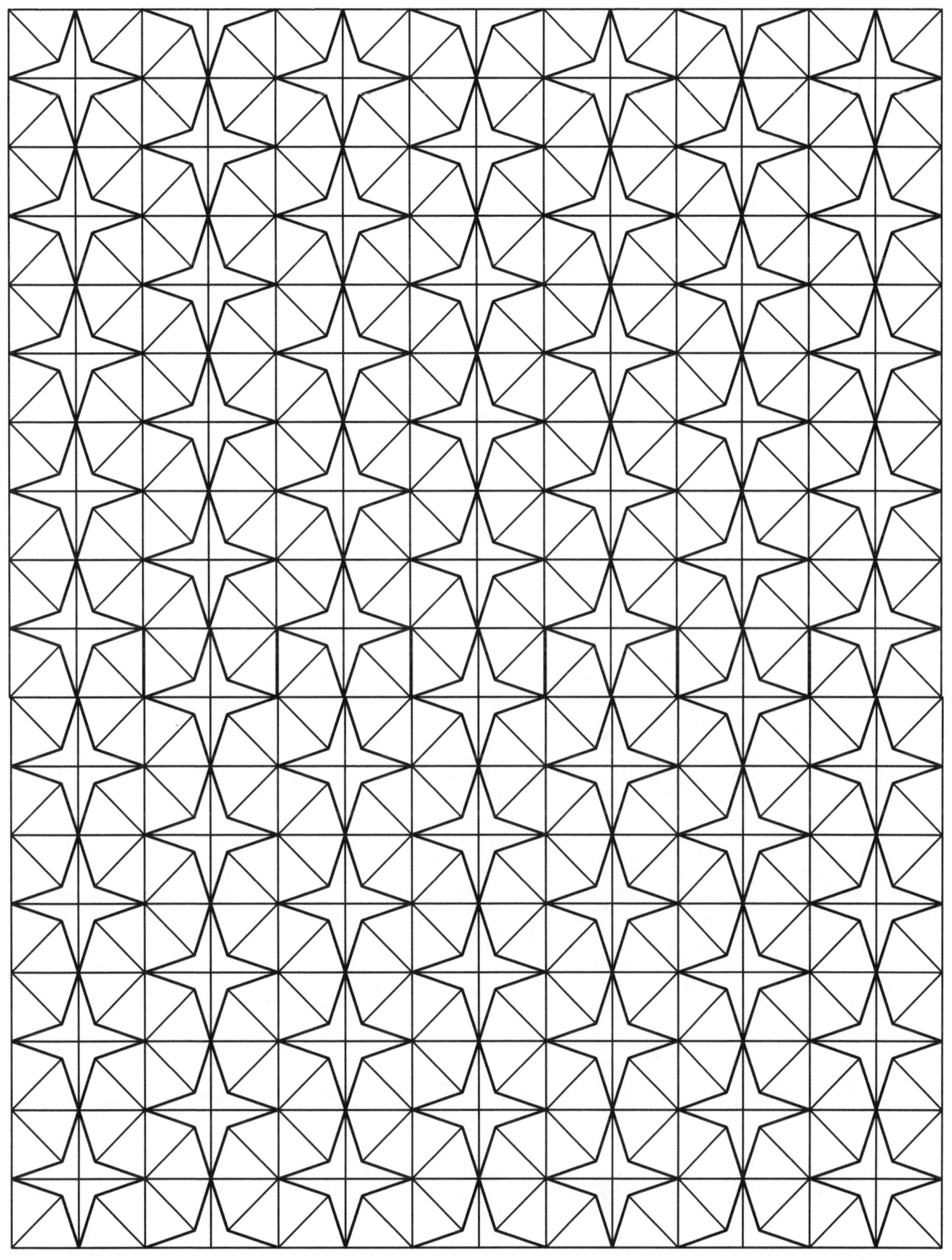

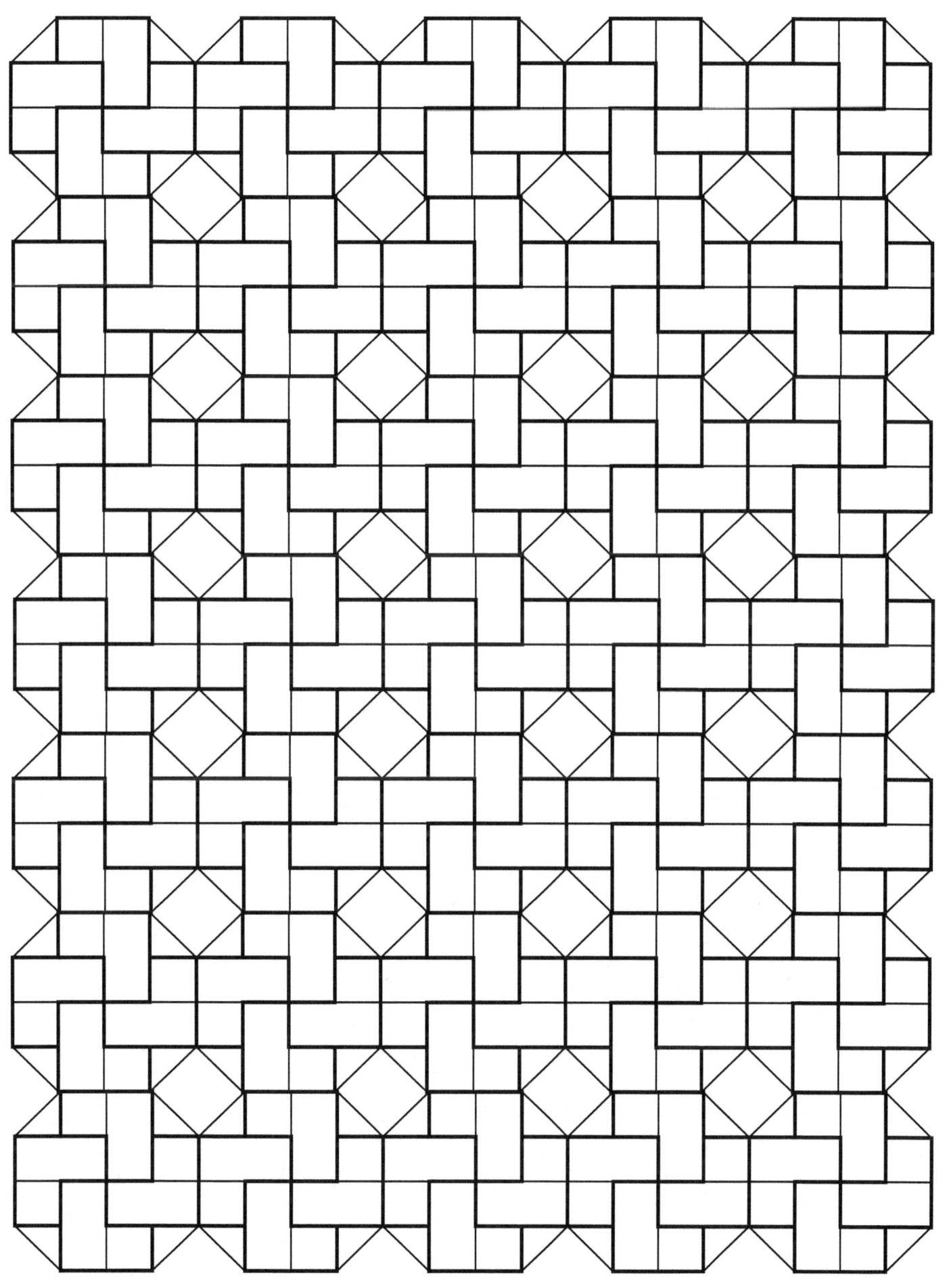

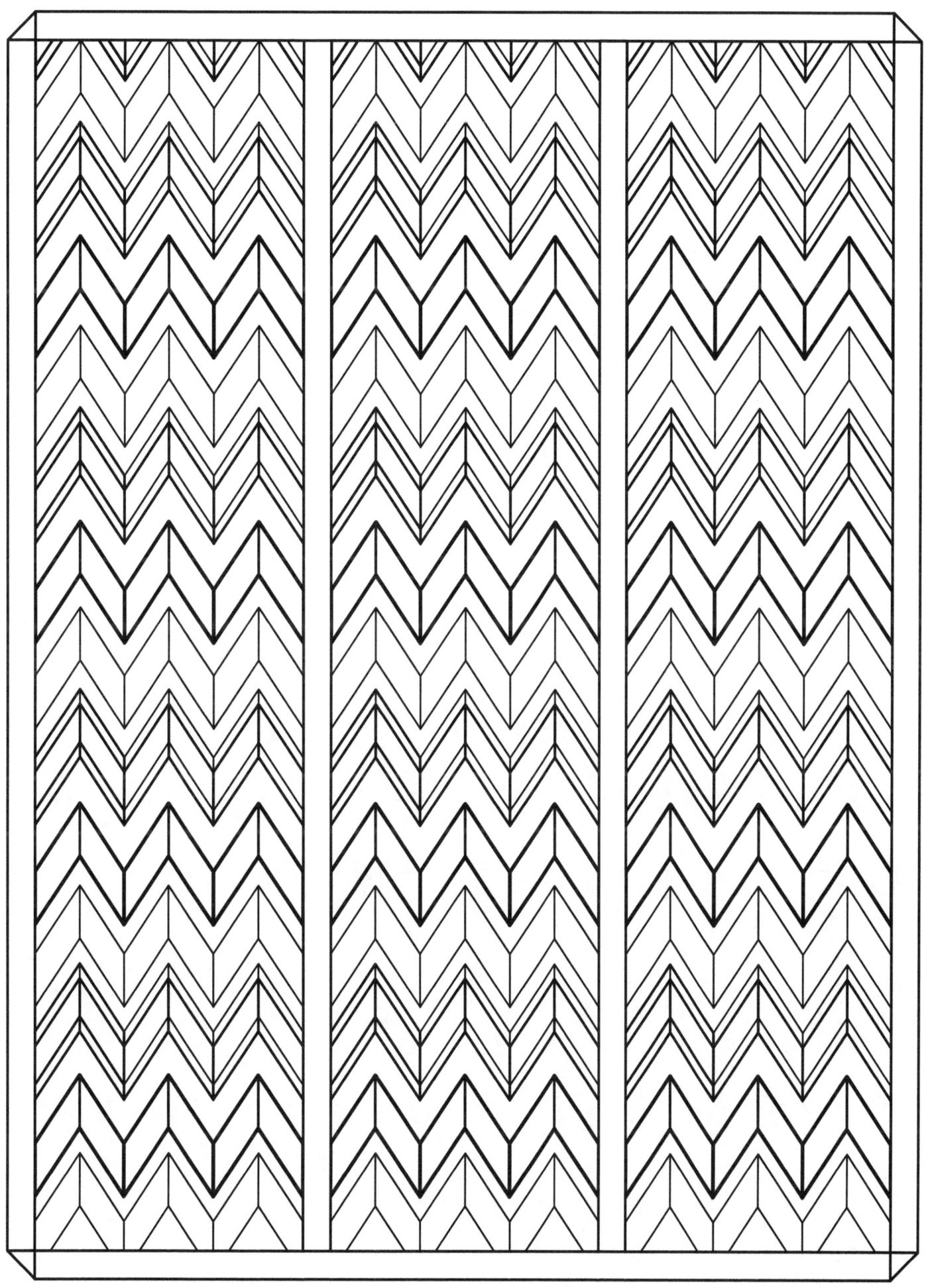

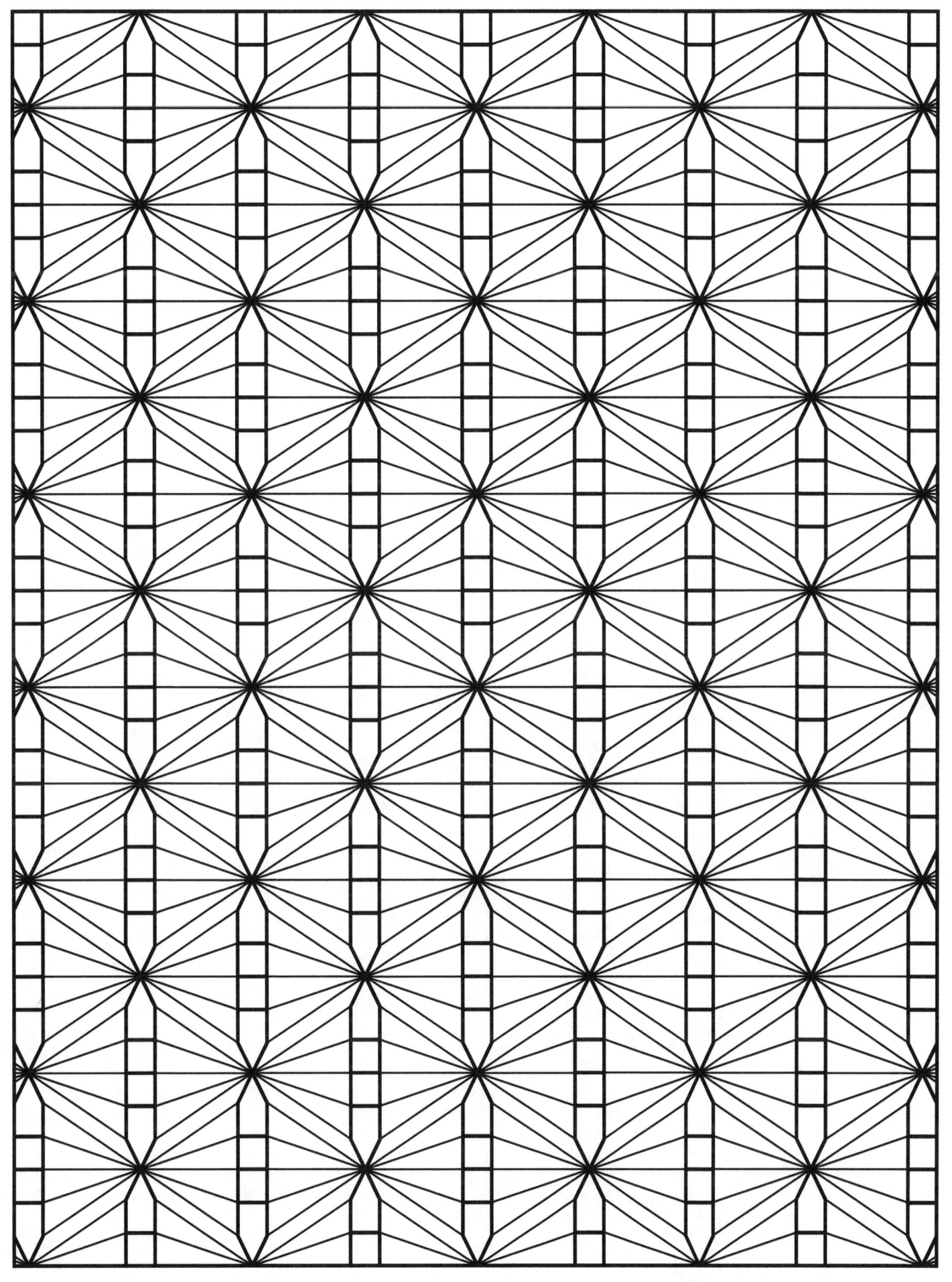

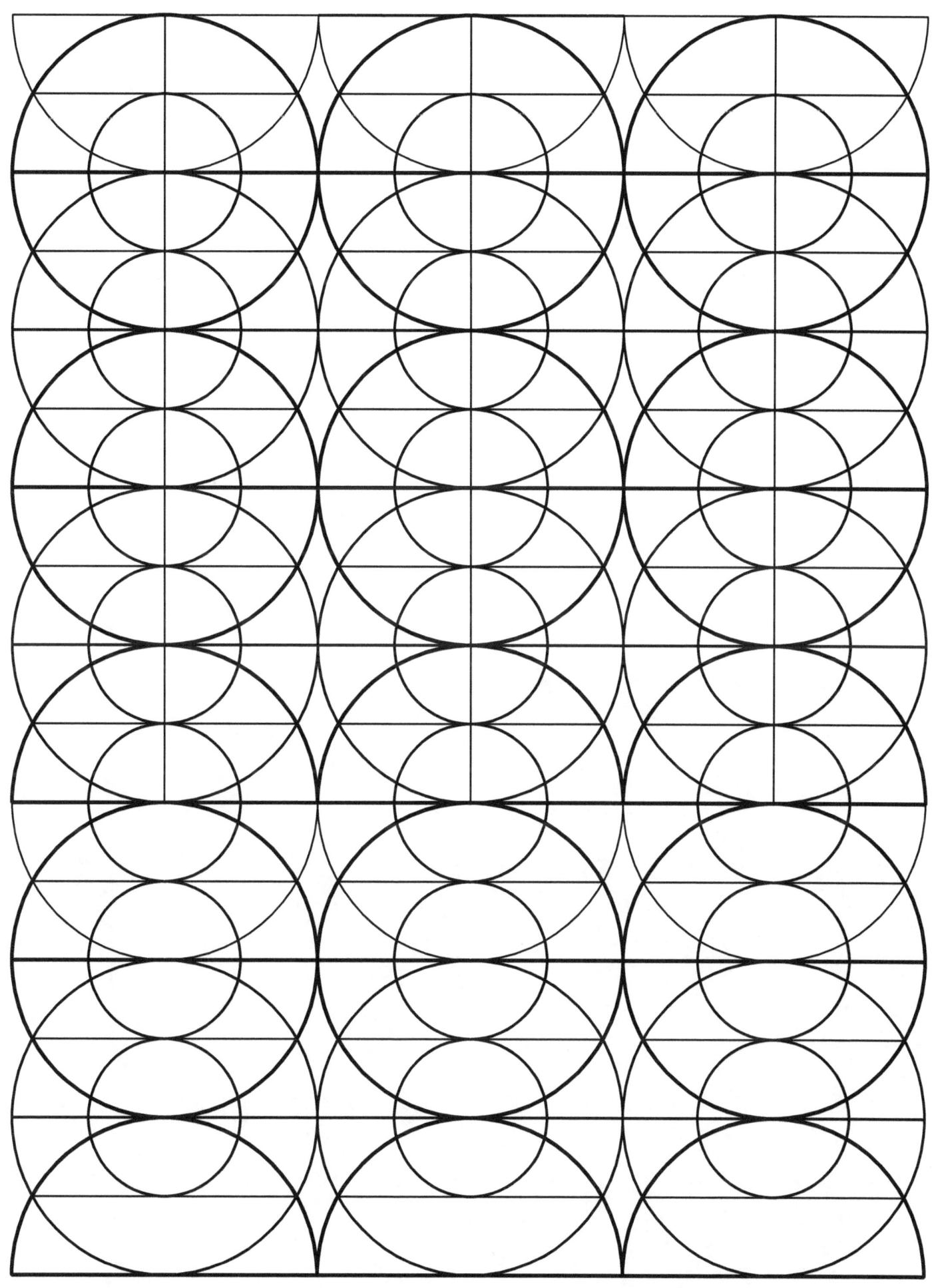

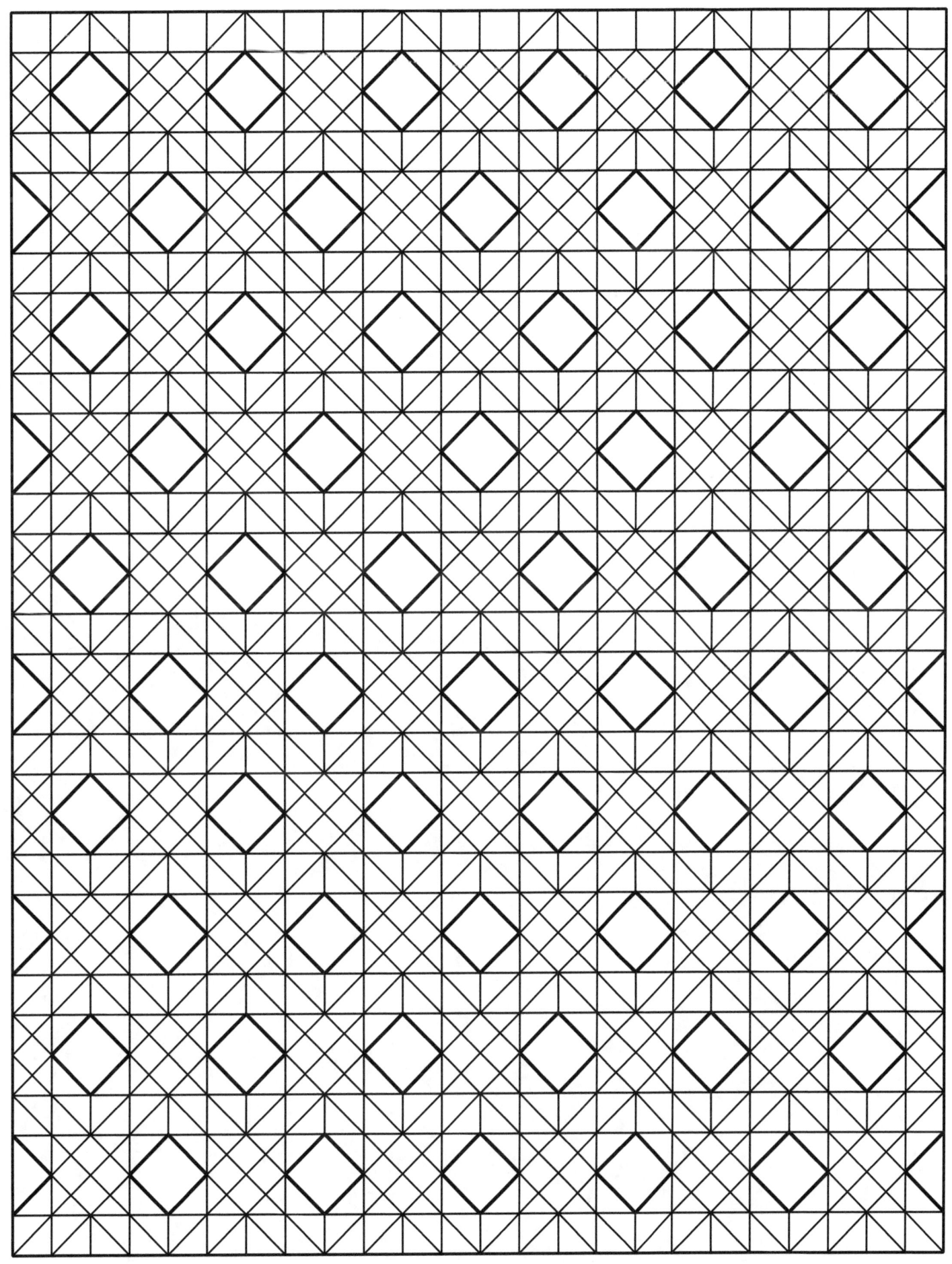

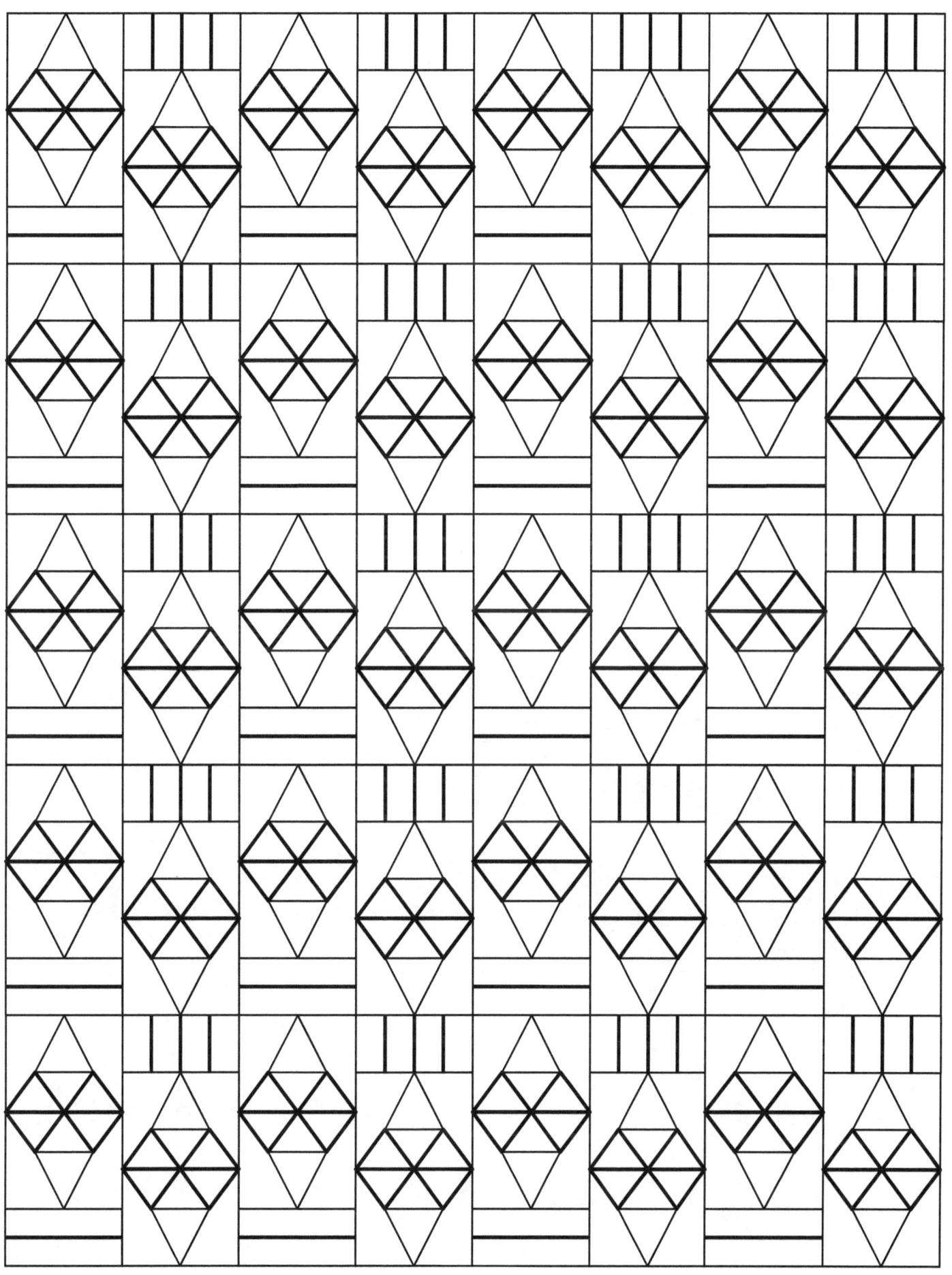

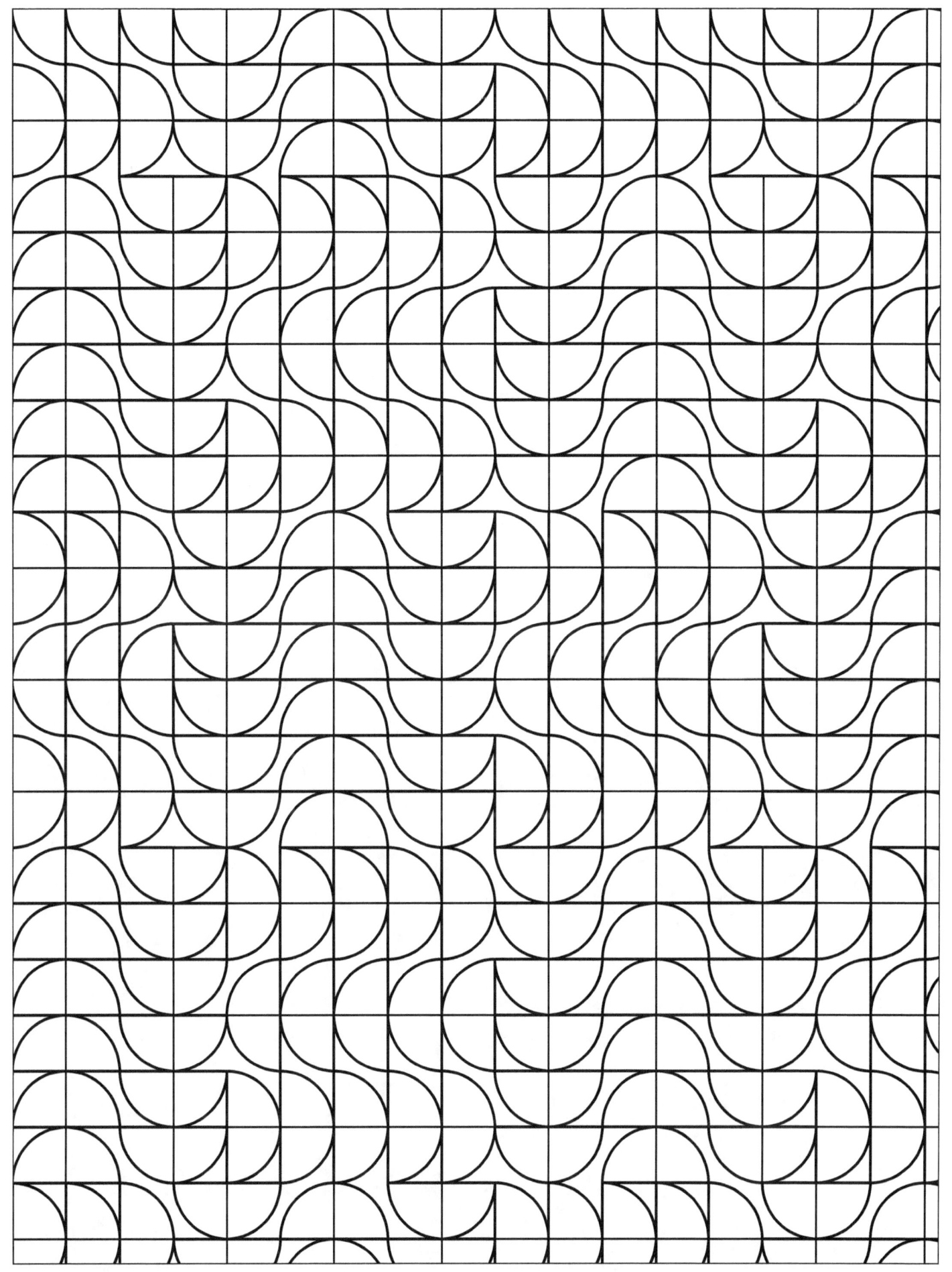

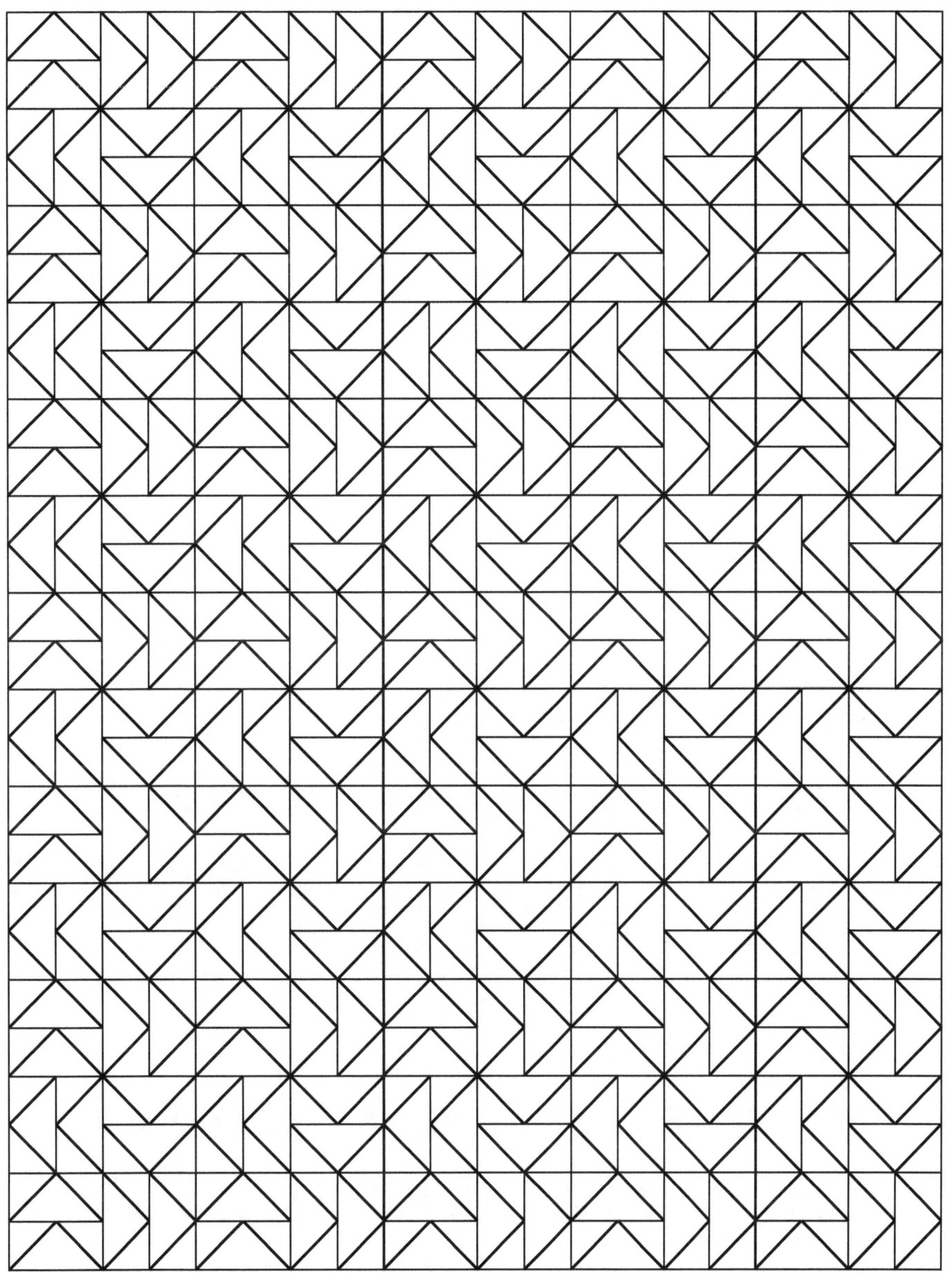

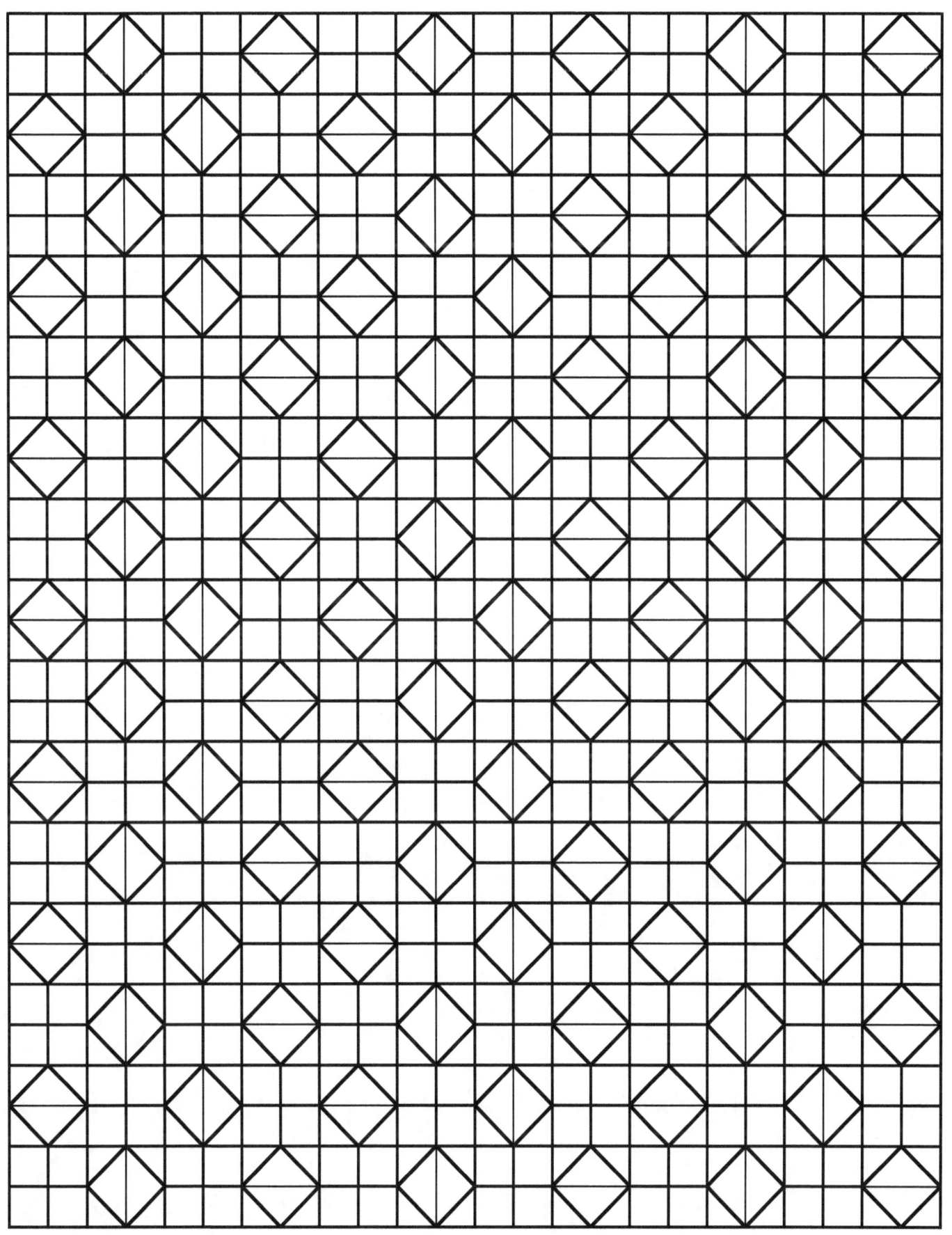

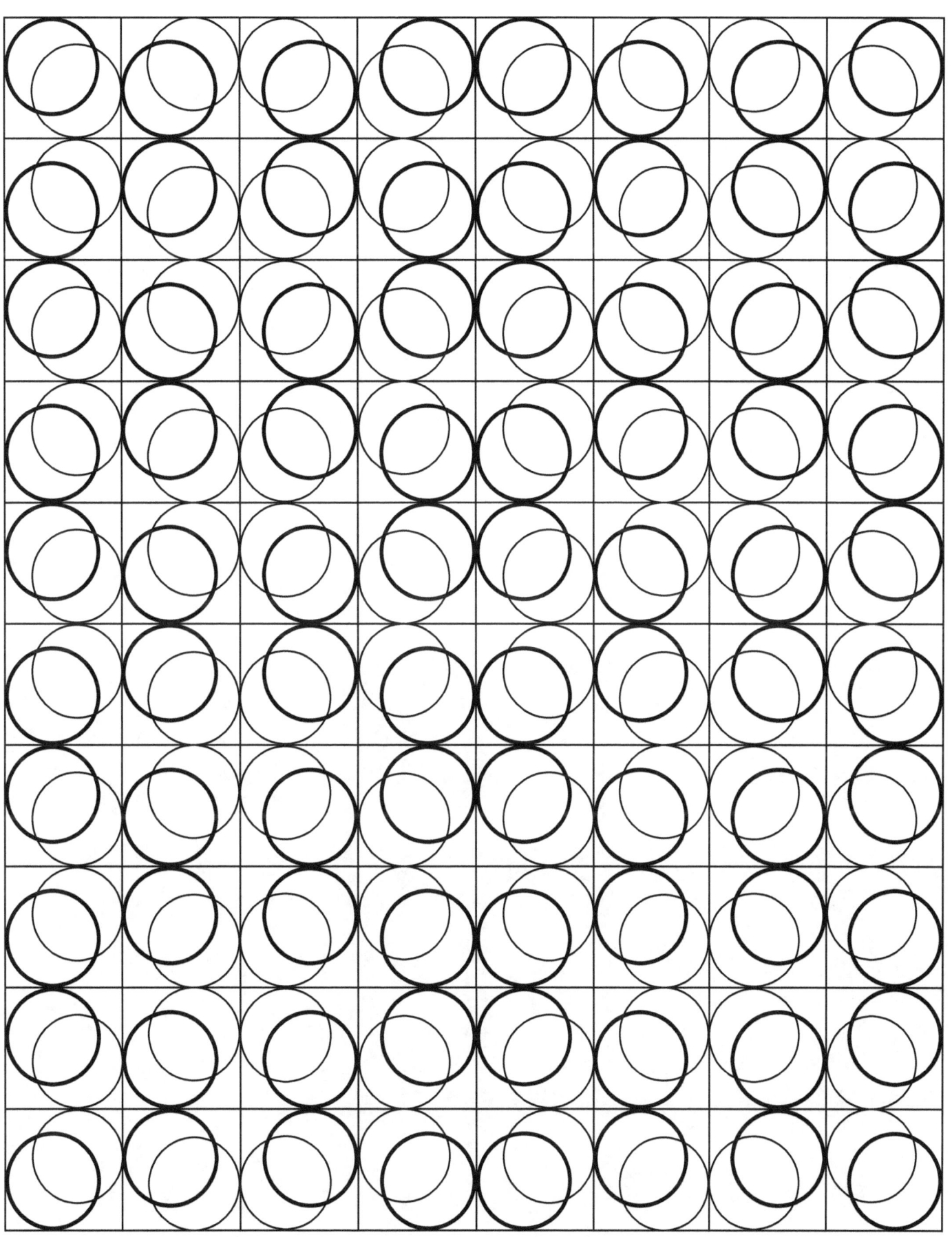

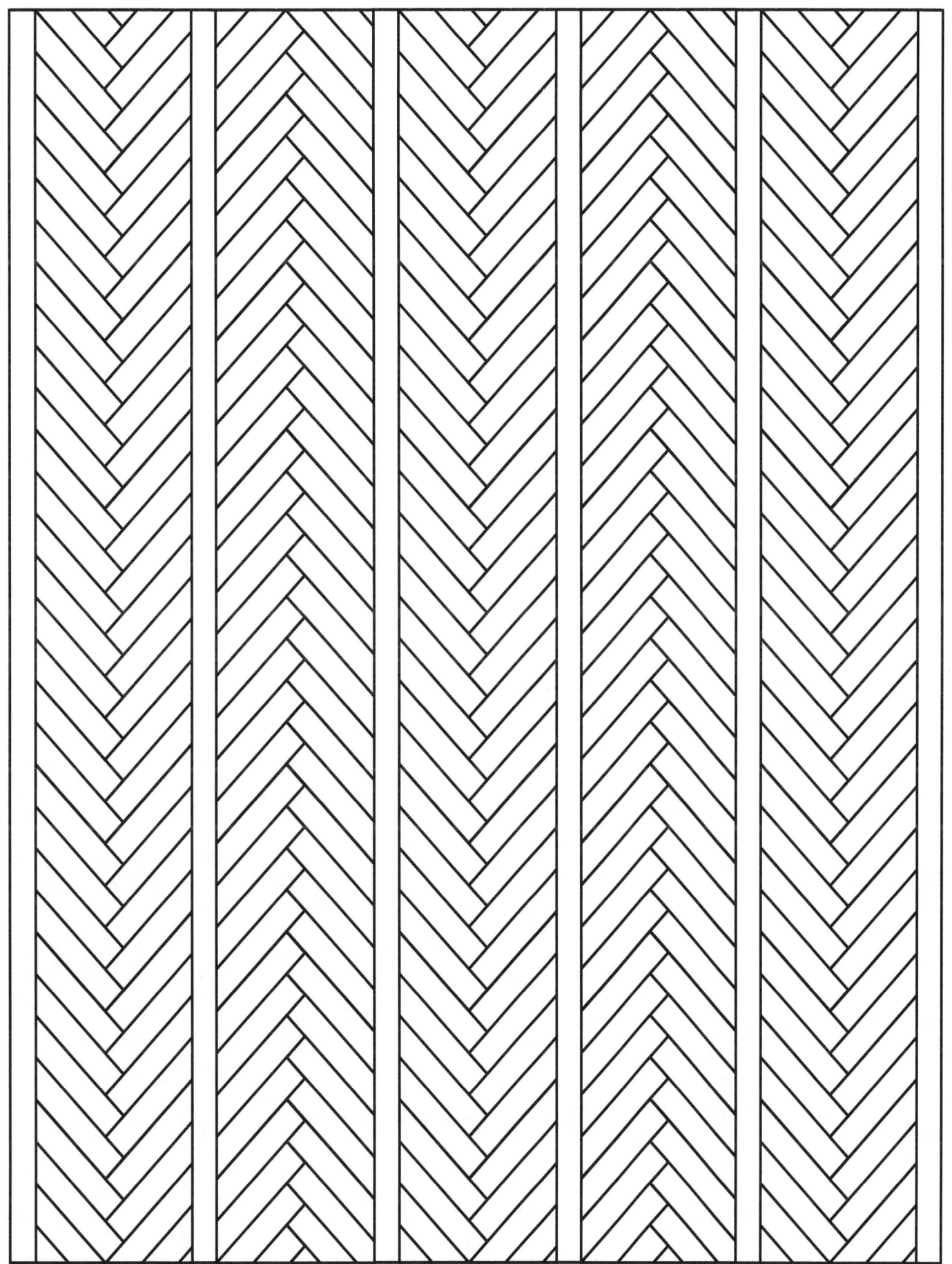

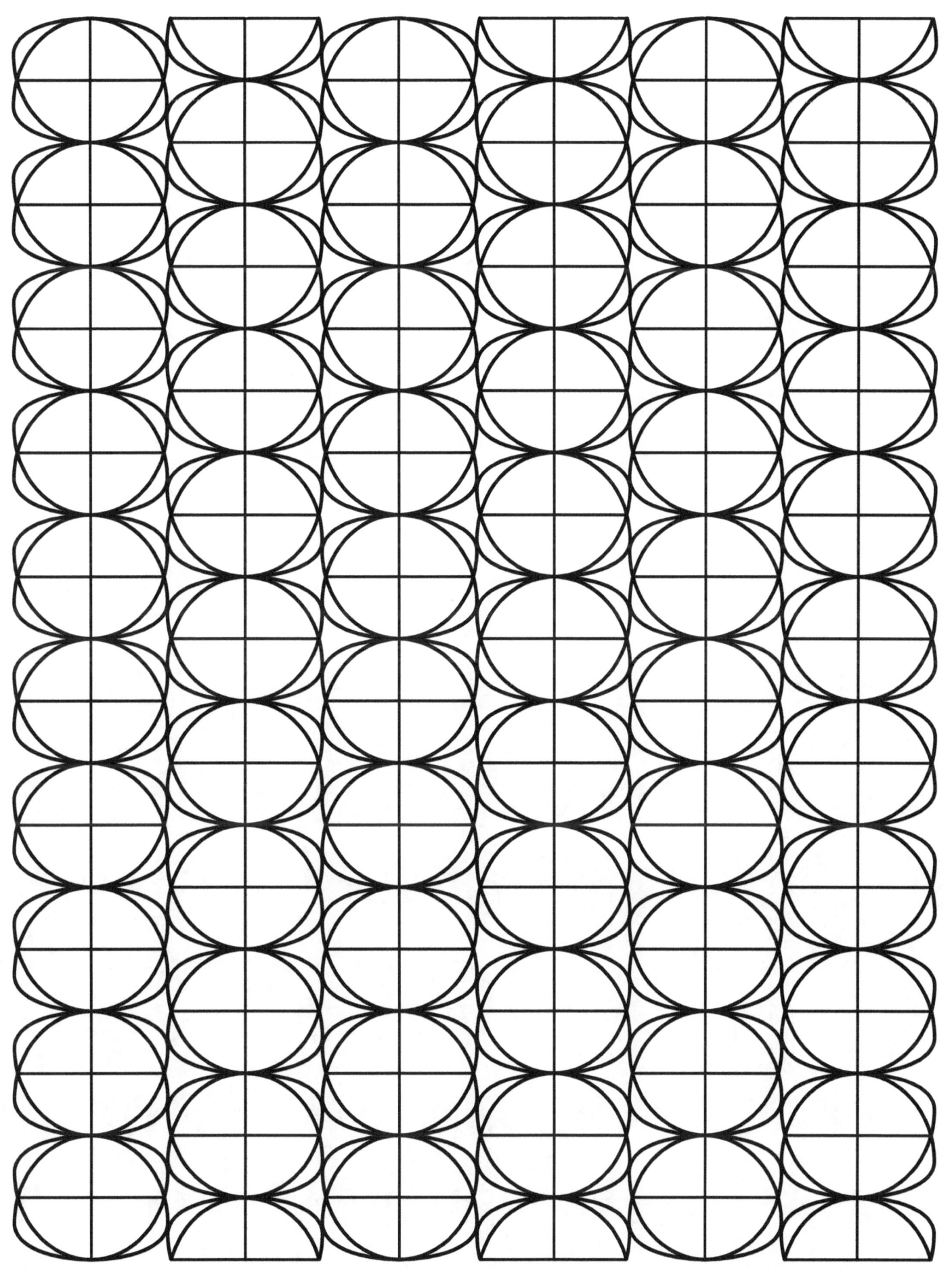

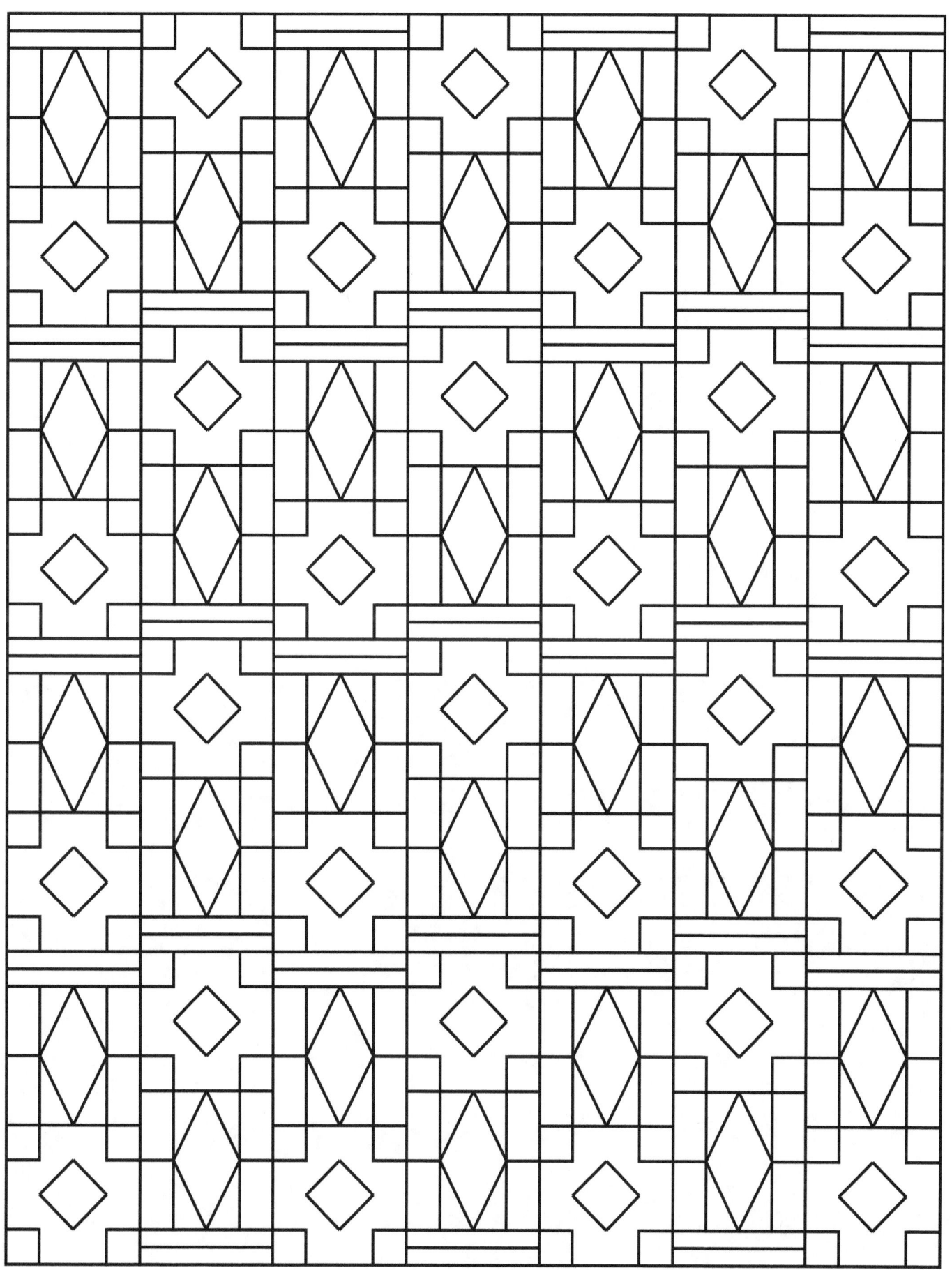

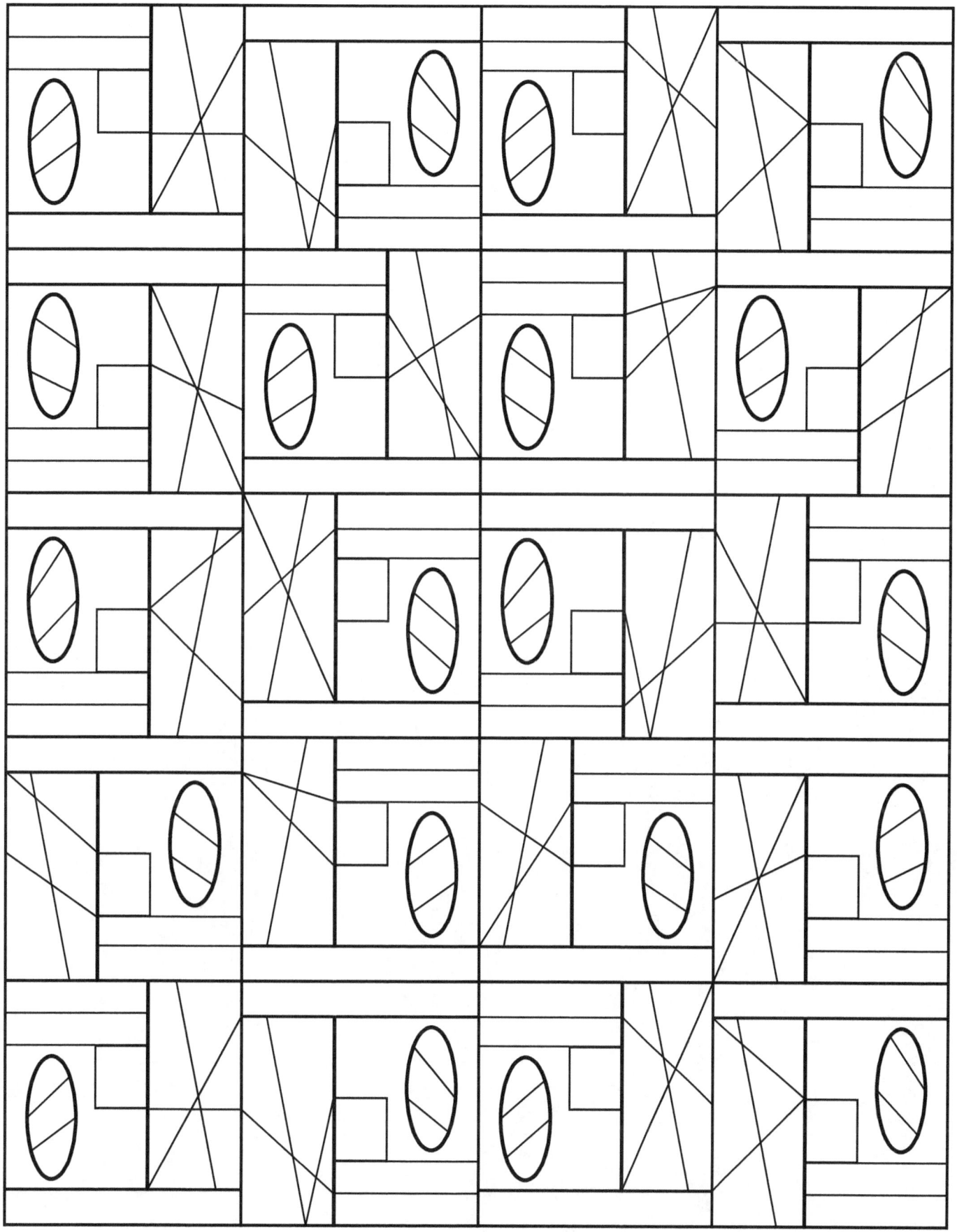

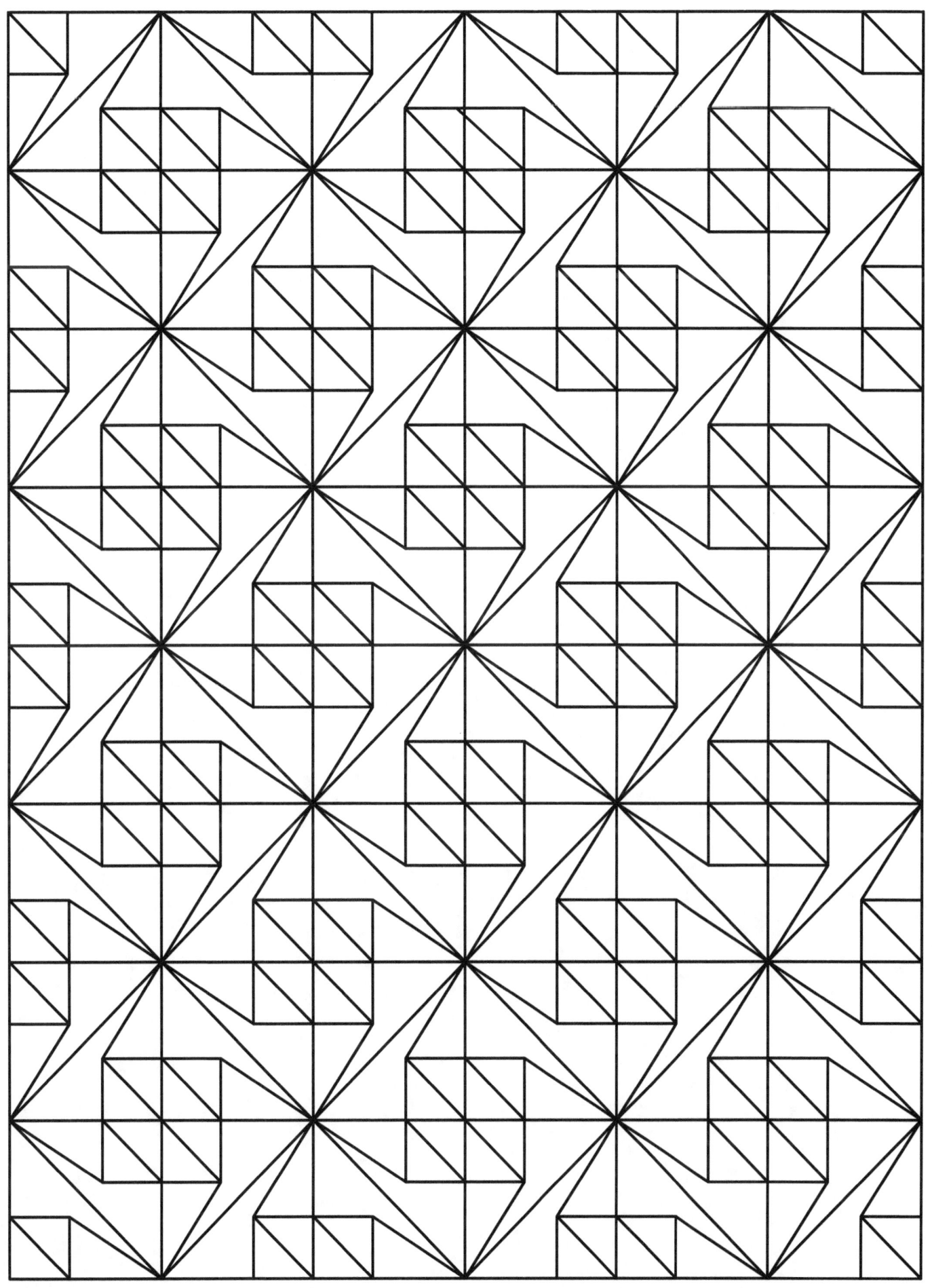

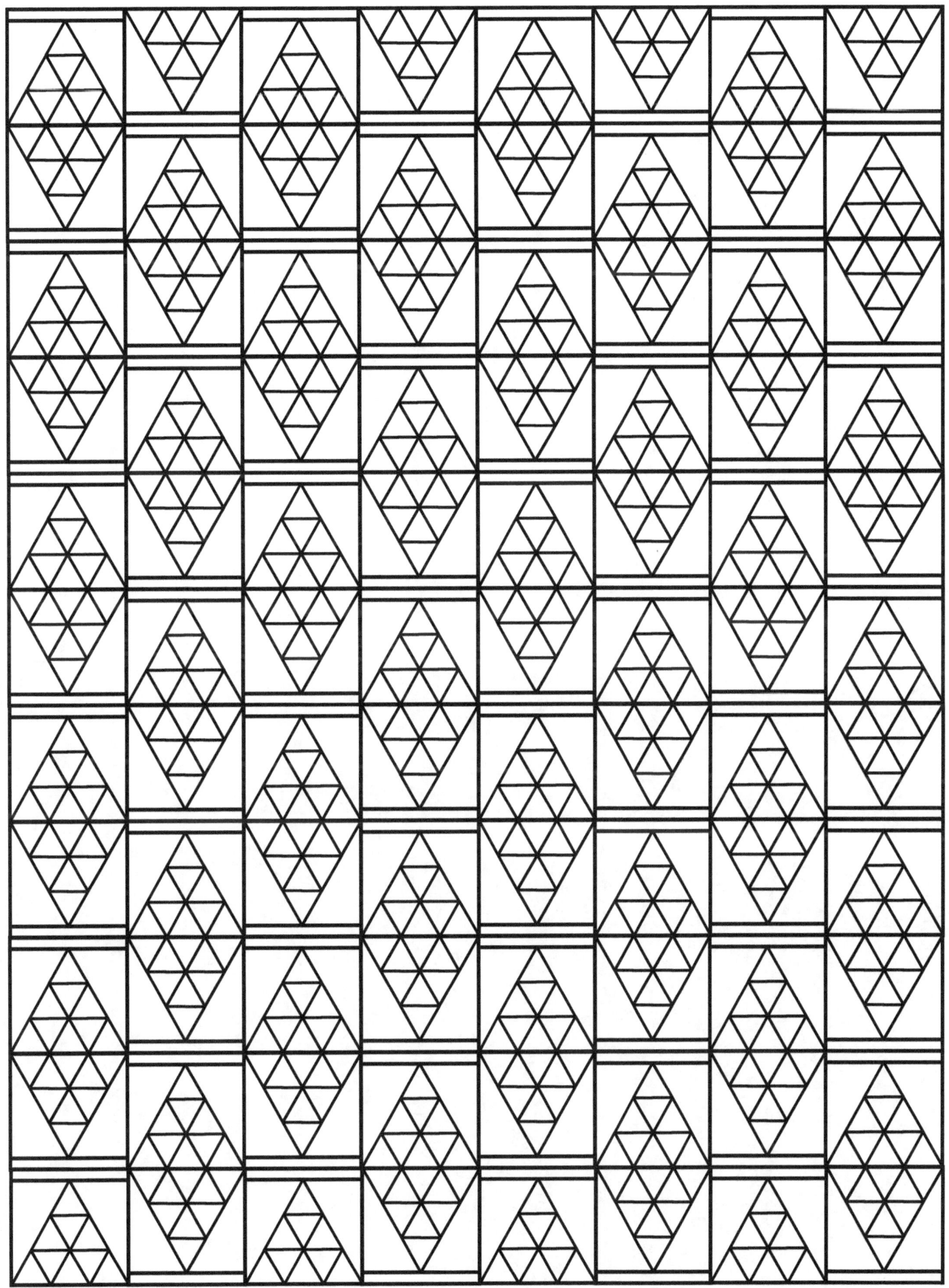

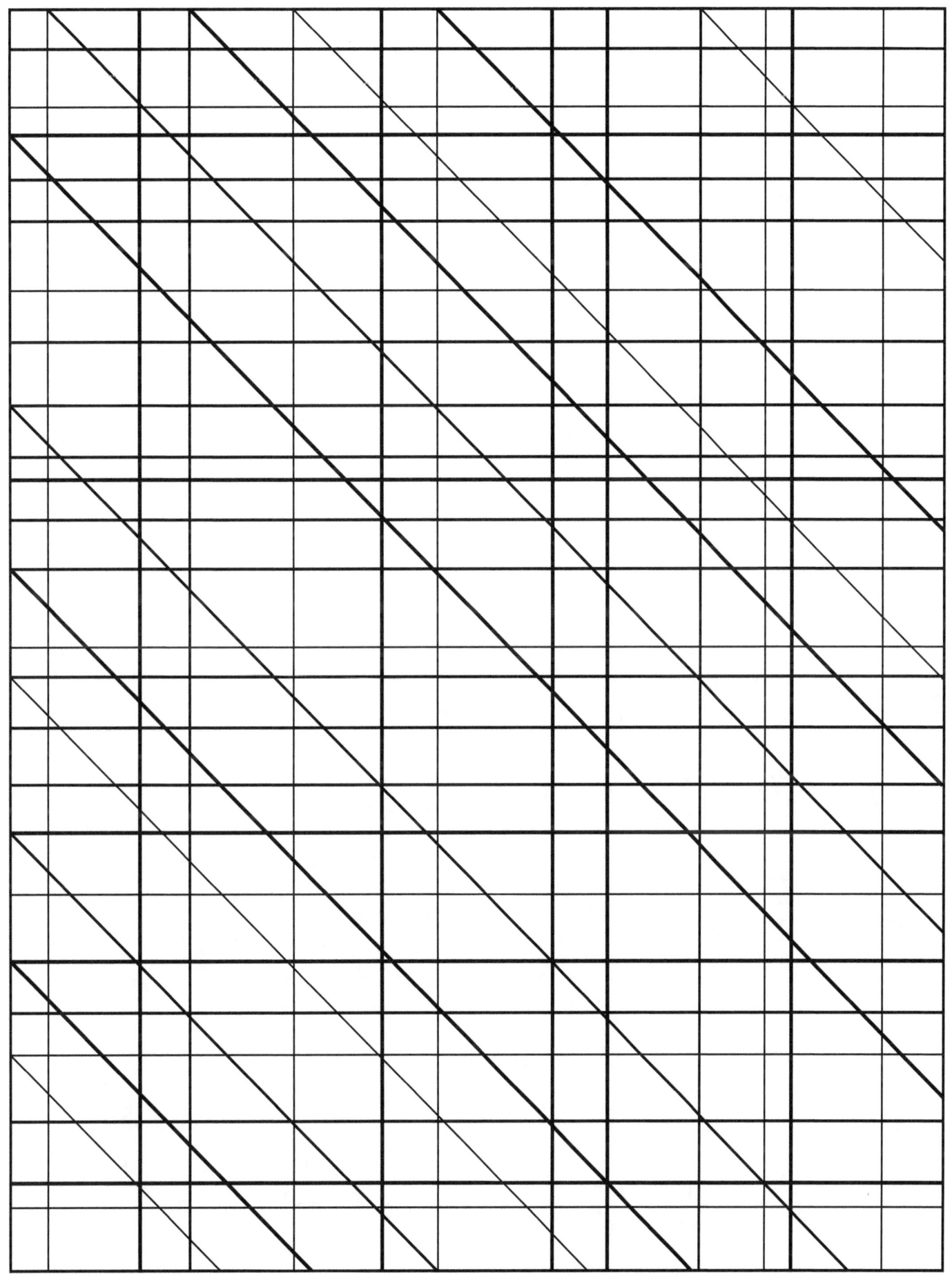

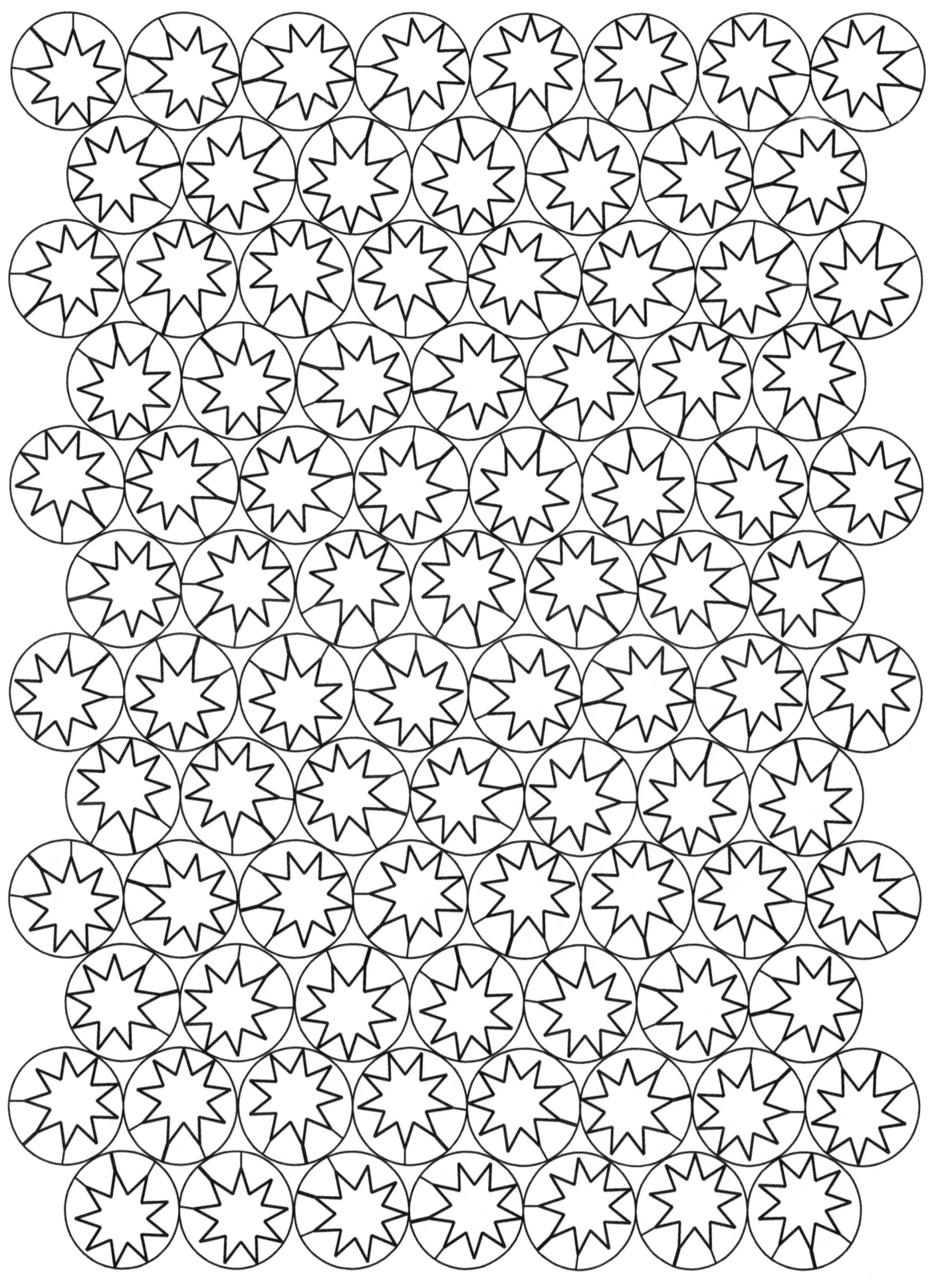

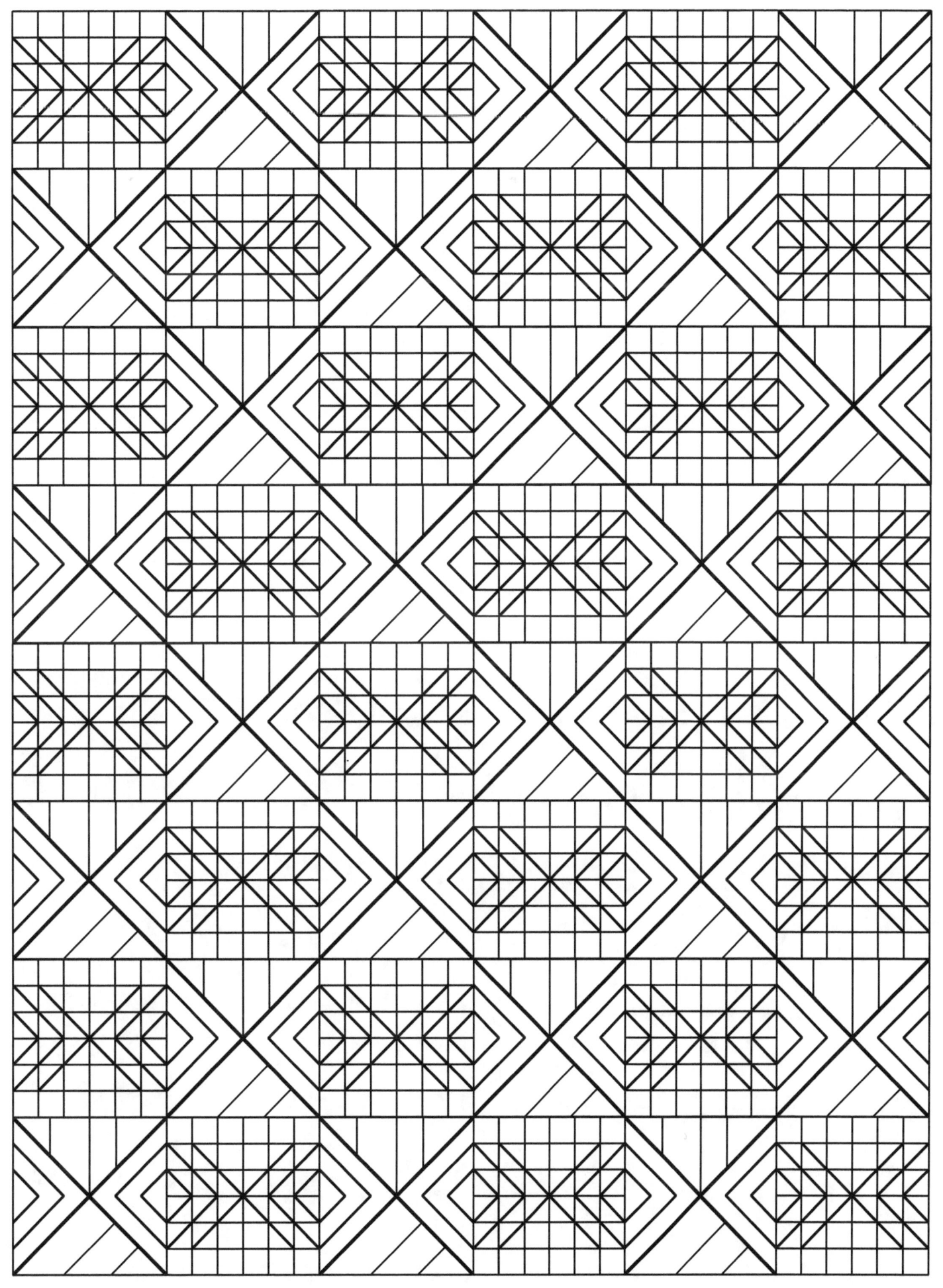

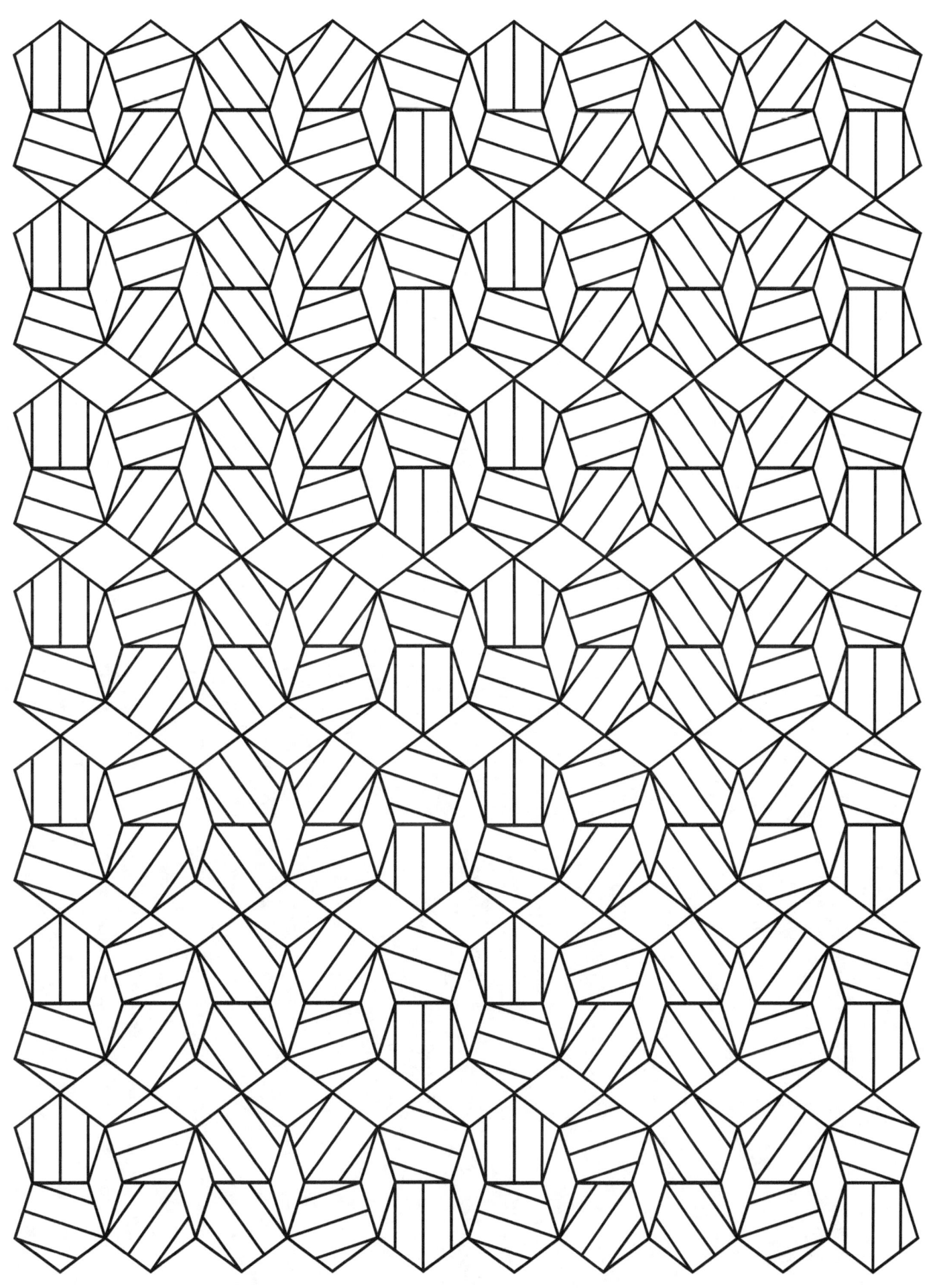

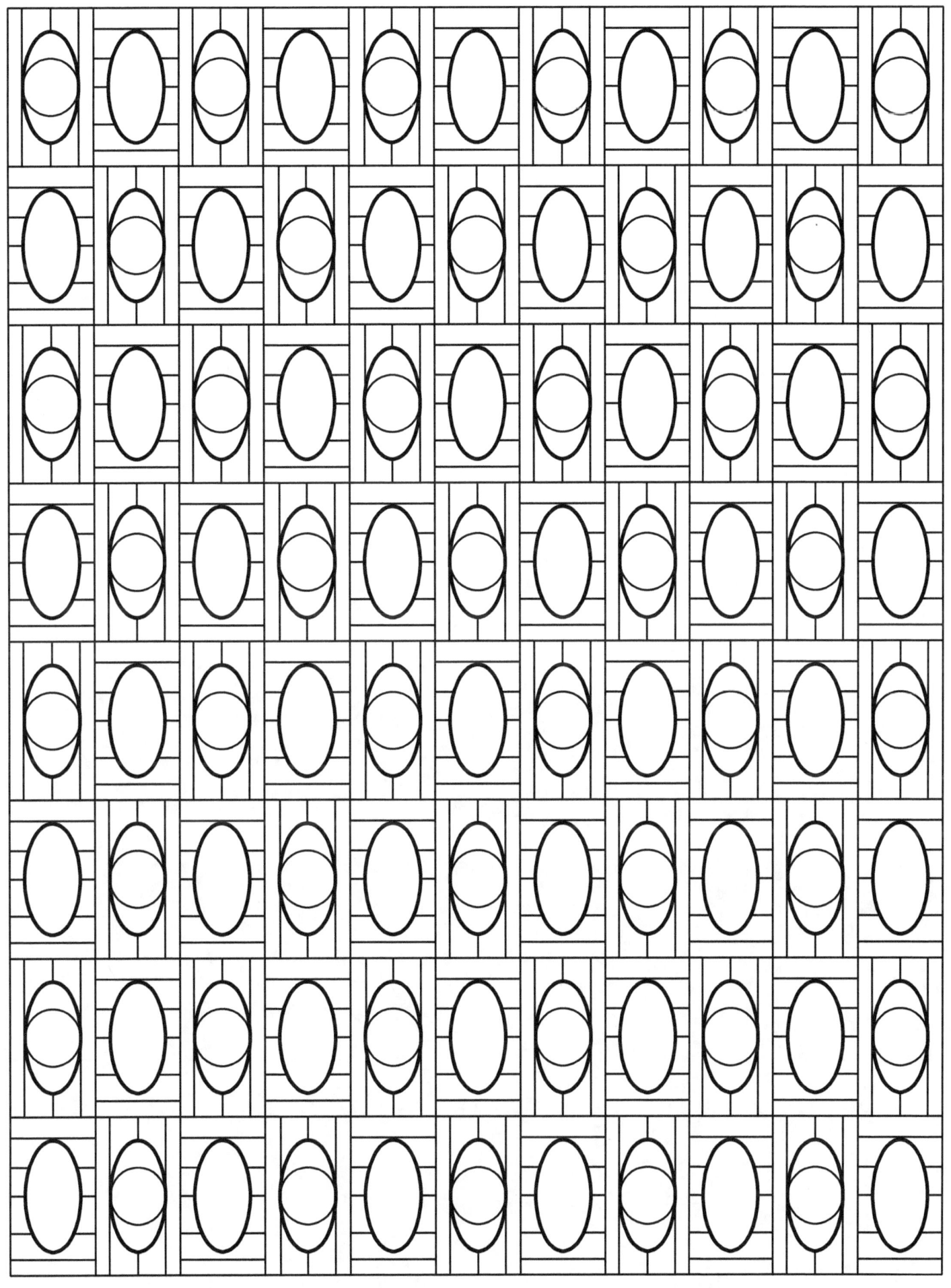

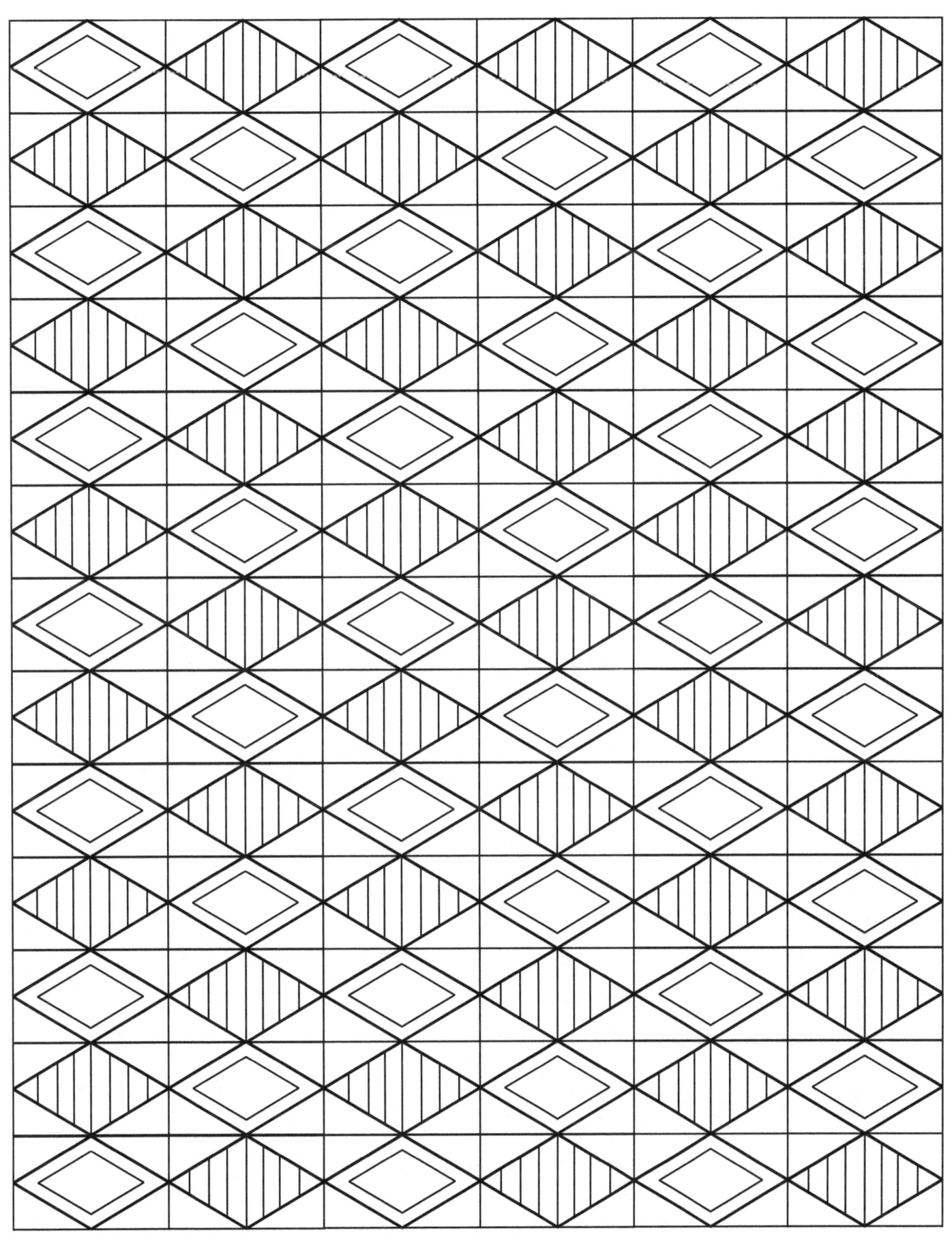

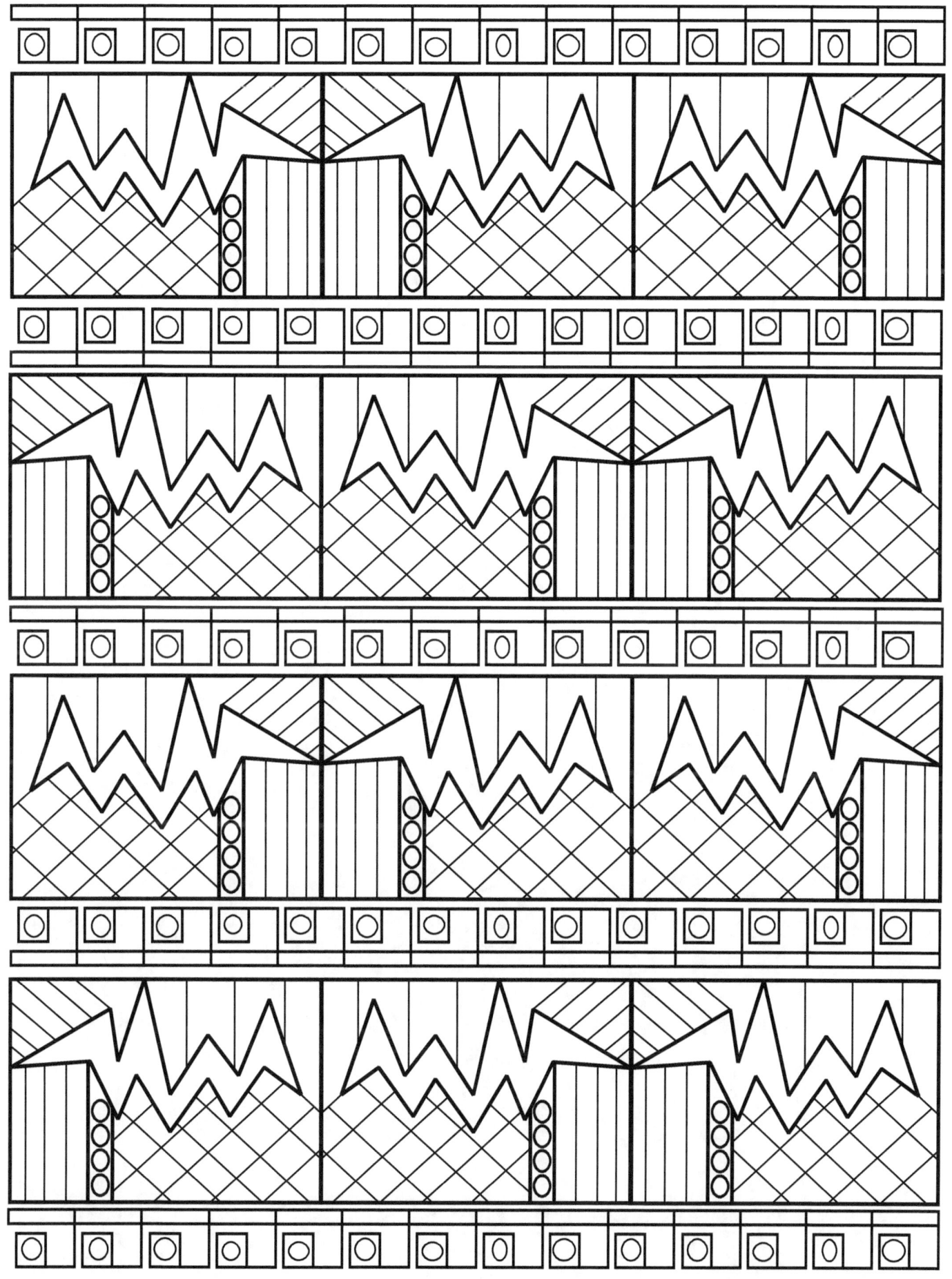

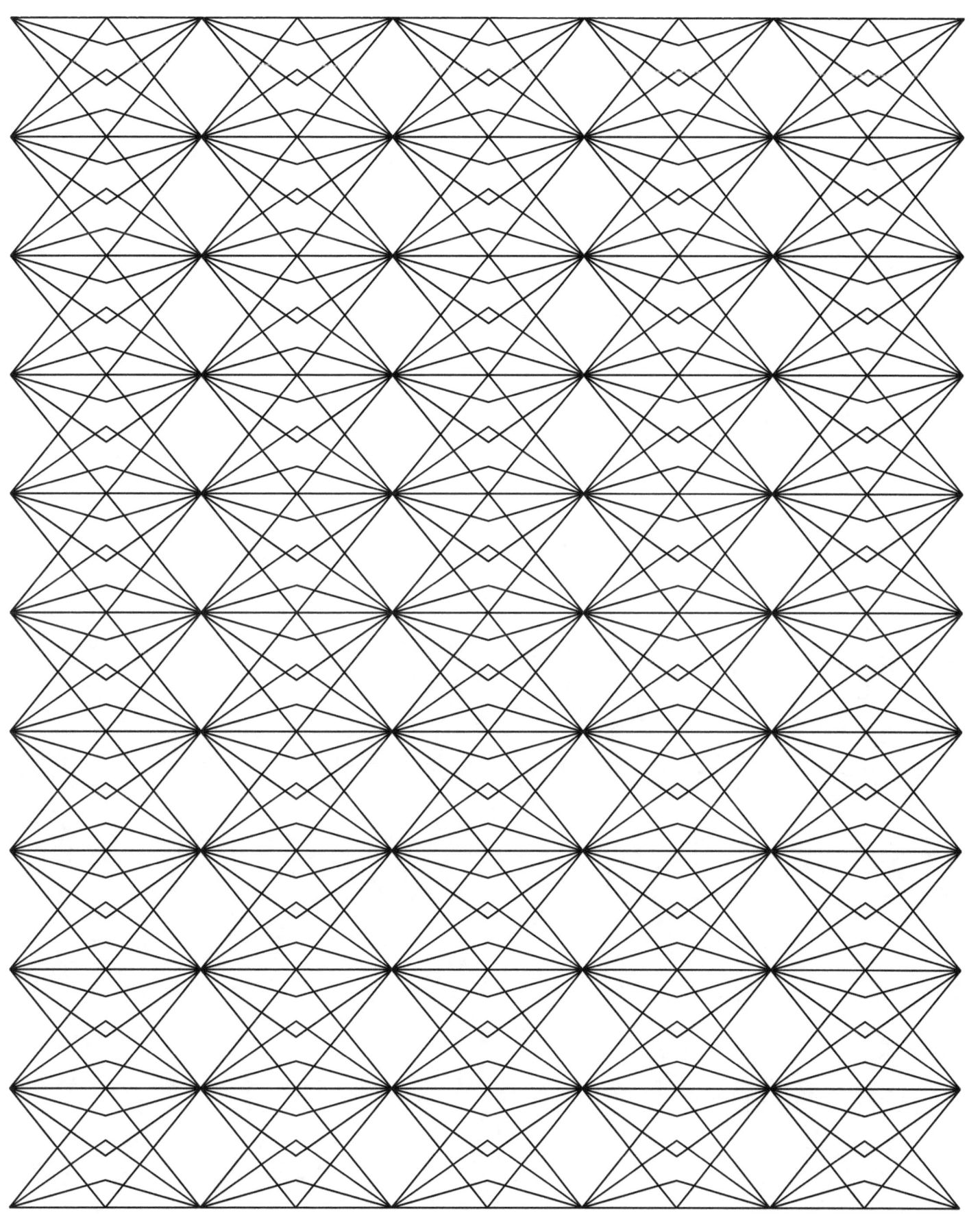

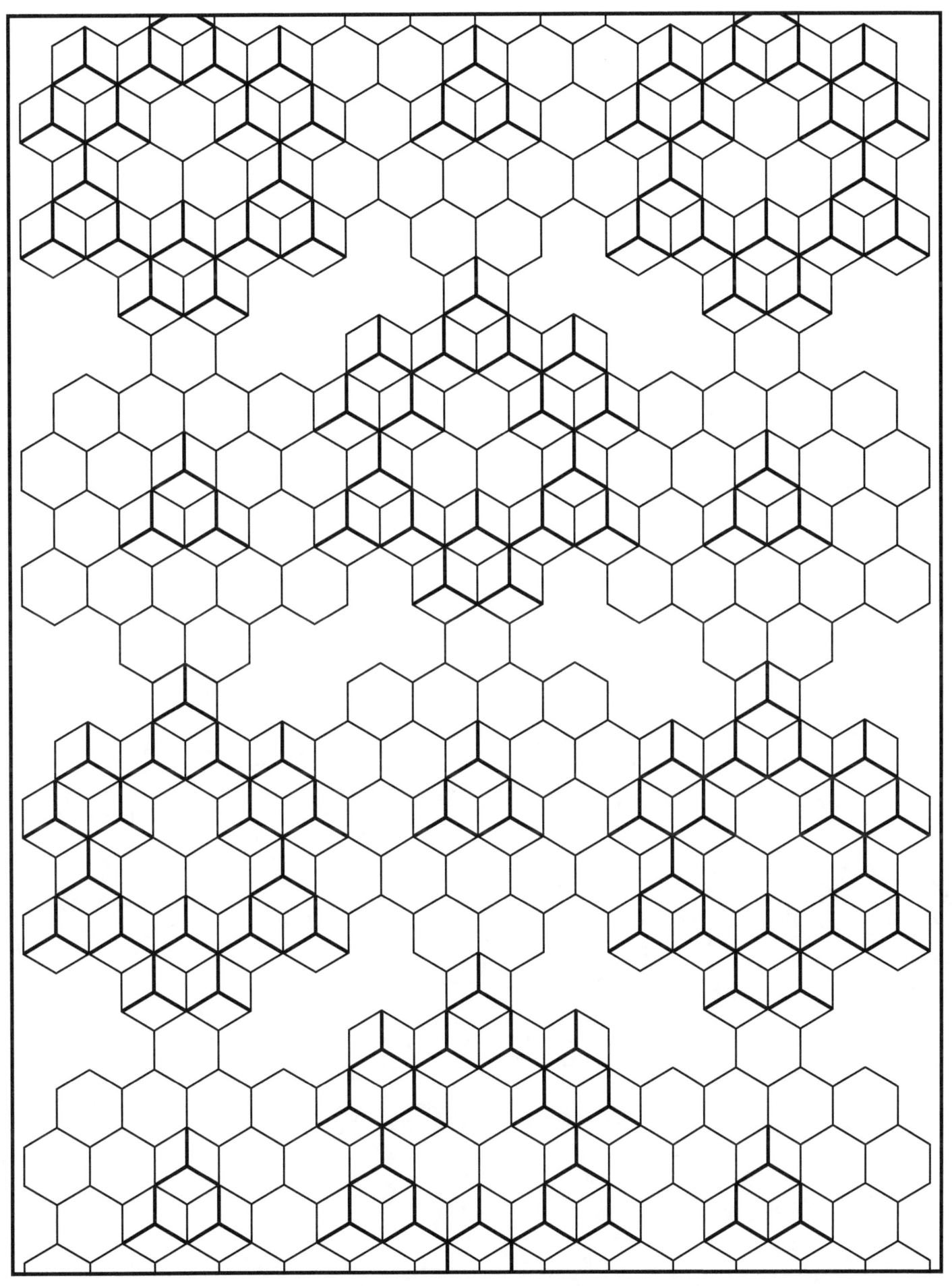

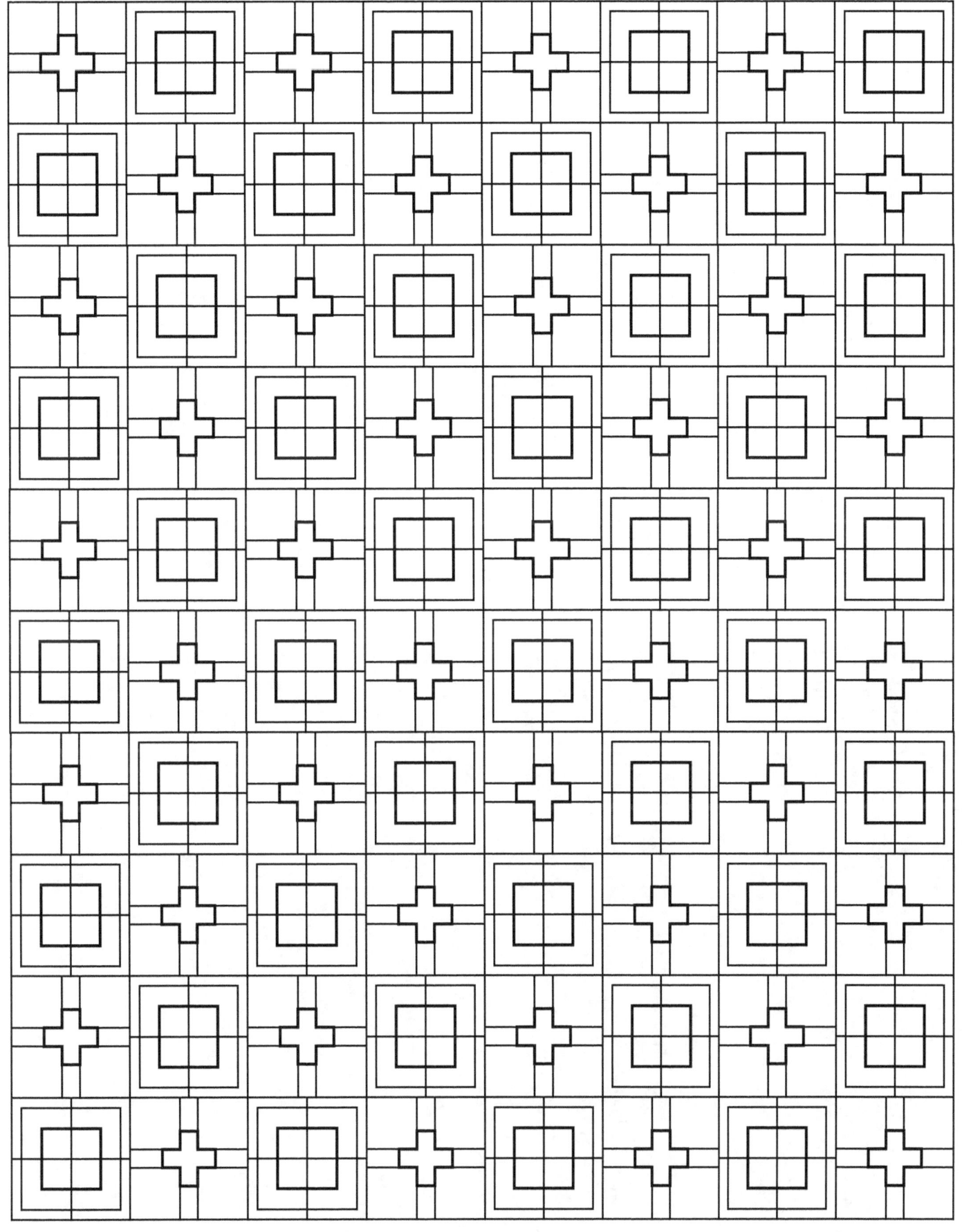

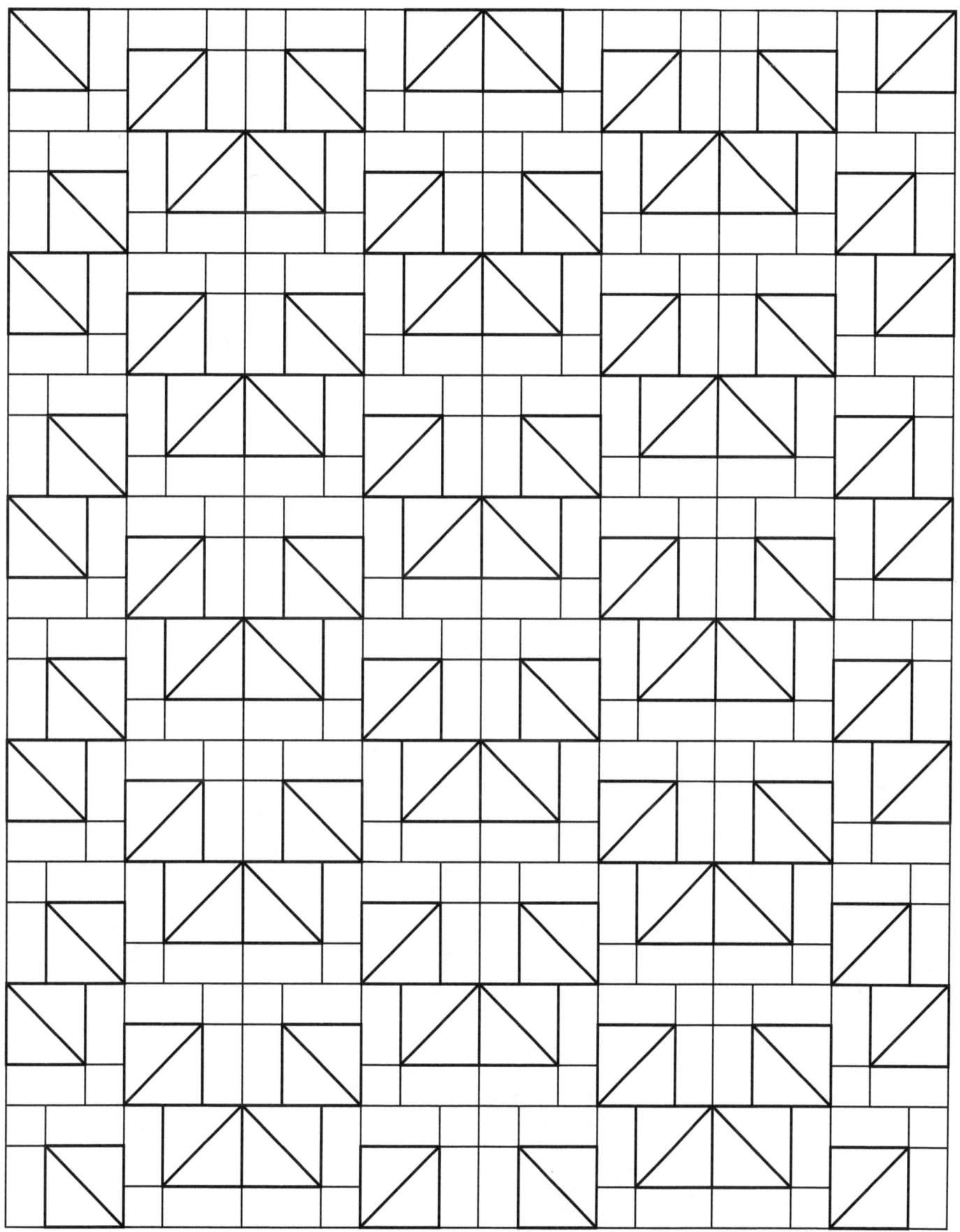

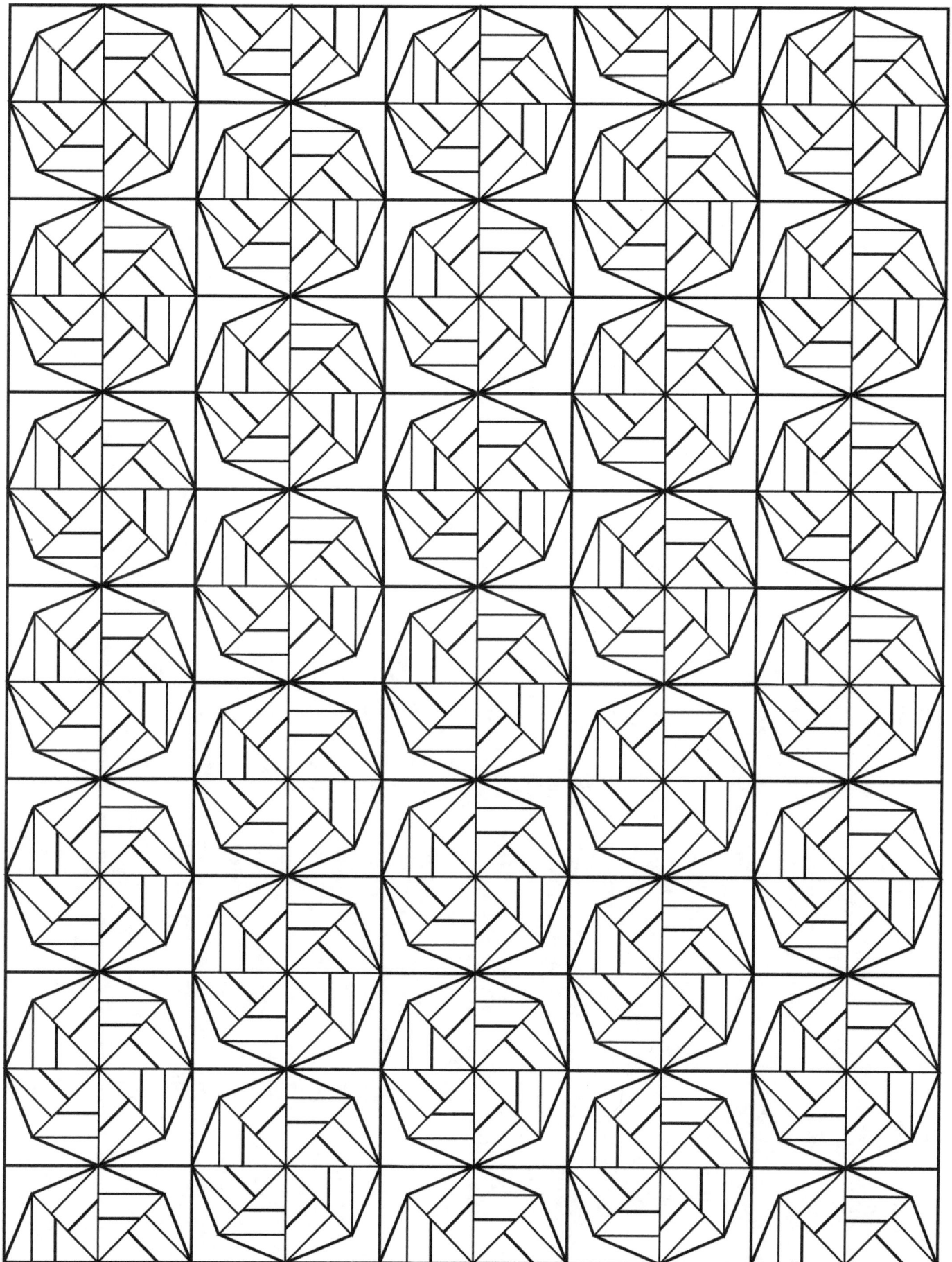